DOMESTIC BROILS

DOMESTIC BROILS

SHAKERS, ANTEBELLUM MARRIAGE, AND THE
NARRATIVES OF MARY AND JOSEPH DYER

EDITED WITH AN INTRODUCTION BY
ELIZABETH A. DE WOLFE

University of Massachusetts Press
AMHERST AND BOSTON

Copyright © 2010 by University of Massachusetts Press
All rights reserved
Printed in the United States of America

LC 2010012377
ISBN 978-1-55849-808-2 (paper); 807-5 (library cloth)

Designed by Sally Nichols
Set in Goudy Old Style
Printed and bound by Thomson-Shore, Inc.

Library of Congress Cataloging-in-Publication Data

Dyer, Mary M., b. 1780.
[Brief statement of the sufferings of Mary Dyer, occasioned by the
society called Shakers] Domestic broils : Shakers, antebellum marriage, and the narratives of Mary and Joseph Dyer / edited and with
an introduction by Elizabeth A. De Wolfe.
    p. cm.
Includes bibliographical references and index.
  ISBN 978-1-55849-808-2 (pbk. : alk. paper) — ISBN 978-1-55849-
807-5 (library cloth : alk. paper) 1. Shakers—Controversial literature. 2. Dyer, Mary M., b. 1780. 3. Dyer, Joseph. 4. Marriage—Religious aspects—Shakers. I. De Wolfe, Elizabeth A., 1961– II. Dyer,
Joseph. Compendious narrative elucidating the character, disposition, and conduct of Mary Dyer, from the time of her marriage, in
1799, till she left the society called Shakers, in 1815. III. Title.
BX9773.D94 2010
289'.808655097409034—dc22

                                                        2010012377

British Library Cataloguing in Publication data are available.

Excerpts from the correspondence of Mills Olcott are used courtesy
of the Dartmouth College Library. The illustrations, Mary Dyer's A
Brief Statement, Joseph Dyer's A Compendious Narrative, and excerpts from "The Mob at Enfield" are used with the permission of
Hamilton College / Burke Library.

To William and Ann Ferrigno
and
Fred and Beverly DeWolfe
on their golden anniversaries

ᕽ

And to the Maine Center for Cancer Medicine
for making golden anniversaries possible

CONTENTS

ILLUSTRATIONS

PREFACE

I first worked with Mary Marshall Dyer's story as a graduate student in American and New England Studies at Boston University. Seeking a paper topic for a course on women and nineteenth-century law and at the behest of my husband, a rare book dealer, I began to read and to take seriously the published works of a woman whose fifty-year campaign against the Shakers most other historians had taken as evidence of mental instability. Instead of the ranting of a frenzied and insane mind, I saw a desperate, and charismatic, woman. I encountered a woman who found herself socially and legally invisible and whose preaching aspirations were fulfilled, ironically, not by preaching *for* a faith but rather by speaking *against* one. As my research into what became my dissertation and later, a biography, deepened, I discovered an intelligent and tenacious woman who was the very linchpin of a loose, but nonetheless organized, anti-Shaker movement.

This collection presents Mary Dyer's first published work, *A Brief Statement of the Sufferings of Mary Dyer* (1818) and the response of her husband, Joseph, who published *A Compendious Narrative* in 1819. Publishers, responding to a frenzy of interest in this private domestic dispute made public, urged customers to "Read Both Sides!" Indeed they did. Reading these two works together presents a unique opportunity to examine one marriage, one family, and one experience with the Shakers from two different perspectives. Touching on issues of the rights and responsibilities of spouses to one another and of parents to their children, the role of print in the new nation, and the limits of religious toleration, the Dyers' texts have relevance two hundred years later, as we continue to debate the "proper" and "best" American family, the credibility of the media, and the presence of alternative religious and secular groups.

The introduction provides background on Shakerism and anti-Shakerism, popular print genres of the day, and divorce practices in the early nineteenth century. The endnotes point the reader to additional sources in these areas. *A Brief Statement*, a thirty-five page pamphlet, was published first in Concord, New Hampshire, and then, as the Dyer debate gained widespread public attention, shortly thereafter in a nearly identical edition in Boston.[1] Mary Dyer's original text is transcribed here from the 1818 Boston edition. Joseph Dyer's *A Compendious Narrative*, an eighty-eight-page pamphlet, was written in 1818, but illness in the printer's family delayed publication until February of 1819. Many surviving copies of Joseph's text indicate (erroneously) 1818 as the date of publication. For chronological clarity, in my discussion of this work I refer to the publication date as 1819.[2] In both cases I have retained the grammar, spelling, and punctuation of the original, except in cases where nineteenth-century punctuation or spelling obscures the meaning, and to correct obvious typographical errors.

An earlier version of the introduction was presented at the New England Historical Association meeting in the fall of 2002 and at the 2004 annual meeting of the Organization of American Historians. Fellow panelists Candace Kanes, Mary Beth Sievens, and Lisa Wilson provided helpful comments and insights from their own work on marital troubles. I'm very grateful for the assistance of Beth Rose Gould, who typed the text of *A Brief Statement*, Cacie Miller Willhoft, who labored with Joseph's *Compendious Narrative*, and Camille Smalley, who proofread and formatted the entire manuscript. Christian Goodwillie, Mary Ann Haagen, and Scott De Wolfe continue to keep me well supplied with fugitive references to Mary Dyer and her much-discussed activities.

Mary Marshall Dyer spent the majority of her life fighting for what she called "the just rights of women." She took particular care in shaping her argument to gain sympathy from women and action from men. That today her words are being read by a new generation of readers—including women who preach, divorce, live as single mothers, undertake careers, and participate in the crafting and passage of laws—would no doubt give her a great deal of pleasure.

DOMESTIC BROILS

INTRODUCTION

*He was one of the best husbands; and I verily believe he would
still have treated me kindly if it had not been for the Shakers.*
Mary Marshall Dyer, *A Brief Statement* (1818)

*I soon found that I must either live in a state of perpetual uproar,
or else condescend to let her do just as she pleased and yield an
implicit obedience to her in all things: and as I always abhorred
quarreling, I submitted to the latter and thought at that time, that of
the two evils I had chosen the least, but I have since doubted it.*
Joseph Dyer, *A Compendious Narrative* (1819)

In August 1819, a desperate woman left a hurriedly scrawled note in
attorney Mills Olcott's kitchen. "If you should hear of my being confined
among the Shakers," Mary Dyer wrote, "I desire you would favor an
afflicted female." Mary had been troubled since 1815, when she abandoned the Shaker sect her entire family had joined just two years earlier.
At one time, Mary thought she had found relief from the relentless labor
of farming and a venue for her religious aspirations in Shakerism, a faith
that allowed women to speak and preach of spiritual matters. But her
dreams went unrealized among the Shakers, and when she left, forced to
leave behind her five children, her dream became a nightmare of social
isolation and legal limbo. Mary had pleaded with her husband, appealed
to town officials, and twice appeared before the New Hampshire state
legislature in an attempt to regain her children and compel her husband, Joseph, to support her. She begged Olcott for protection from
Joseph's power to control the children and deny her assistance. She
explained what her life had become: "The ties from my heart to my dear
children causes me to . . . appear among strangers that I may be near to
them—and now I find myself under that imbarisment that I have been
willing to appear in your kitchen."[1]

Today the Shakers are considered models of simple living and em-
blematic of the religious, agricultural life of days gone by, but in the early
decades of the nineteenth century, when Mary Dyer feared the Shakers
would cause her death, the public looked on them with suspicion, and
their faith and practices challenged other New England Protestants.
The movement was founded in England by a charismatic young woman,
Ann Lee, but in 1774 Lee and a group of followers came to the United
States, gathering first in Niskeyuna, New York, just outside Albany. By
the end of the eighteenth century Lee had passed on, but she left a faith
that had grown to over thirteen hundred members living in eleven communal villages. At their peak in the 1840s the Shakers would count over
four thousand members in eighteen communities from New England
west to Ohio, Kentucky, and Indiana.[2] In the first half of the nineteenth
century, the public slowly came to accept Shakerism as a legitimate,
though perhaps misguided, faith. Nonetheless, with their practices of
celibacy, communalism of goods, and confession of sin, the Shakers
found themselves the frequent subject of inquiry and controversy. Yet
they did not sit idly by as their faith and practices were attacked; they
fought back in courts, in front of the legislature, and in print. One of
their greatest battles was waged with Mary Dyer, a contest that would
span half a century. In her quest to retrieve her five Shaker-held children and to argue for what she called "the just rights of women," Mary
published five books outlining the dangers Shakerism presented to individuals, to families, and, indeed, to the nation. Her husband, who
remained a Shaker, responded in kind, defending his new communal
home and attacking his estranged wife in a book of his own.

Reading Mary's and Joseph's works together allows us to observe
Shakerism, and a marriage, from connected yet opposing points of view.
The Dyers' dueling accounts riveted their readers with details of a marriage falling apart set against the backdrop of a celibate, sectarian faith
that erased the marital bond. Their texts invited the public into two
previously private domains: the domestic space of the marriage and the
sacred space of the secluded Shaker village. Escaping to or escaping
from Shakerism, Joseph and Mary offered to a court of public opinion
their personal and marital stories, and these texts challenged readers to
debate what was worse for society, bad marriages or, in a society like the
Shakers, no marriage at all.

The Dyers' marriage was likely troubled from the start. In 1799 the Reverend Selden Church joined together nineteen-year-old Mary Marshall and Joseph Dyer, a twenty-seven-year-old widower with a young son. Mary had grown up in northern New Hampshire, in a newly settled area that still feared Indian attacks. Independent, self-educated, and ambitious, the young wife expected to have a voice in family decisions and management. The transition from youthful girl to married woman was apparently difficult, and Mary found it hard to settle into the routine of child-care and housework. Joseph had been raised in Connecticut, in an area thickly settled and well established; his world was one of order, routine, and hierarchy, attributes he expected in his marriage. With money inherited from his father's estate, Joseph had left Connecticut for the frontier of New Hampshire in the mid-1790s. He established a home in Stratford, married for the first time, and had a son, Mancer. Joseph was widowed sometime before 1798, and a year later he married Mary Marshall.

The partnership did not go well: Mary criticized Joseph's drinking and card-playing; Joseph decried his wife's volatile temper and sharp tongue. Both felt a call to preach, but not with each other. When Mary left home to lead a meeting, Joseph complained that he was forced to care for the children, who by 1809 included the couple's four sons and one daughter in addition to Mancer. When Joseph preached, Mary felt trapped at home. The Dyers' lives took a fateful turn in 1811 when Lemuel Crooker, an itinerant preacher, visited their home, now in Stewartstown, New Hampshire. He brought news of an intriguing new faith: Shakerism. Despite warnings from their neighbors, who had heard strange stories about Shakers, the Dyers and Crooker traveled to the nearest Shaker community, in Enfield, New Hampshire, nearly a hundred miles to the south. They stayed the weekend learning about the faith, its practices, and the people called Shakers.

Despite the Dyers' initially positive experience at the Enfield community, their newfound interest in Shakerism seemed only to exacerbate the tensions already present in their marriage. For the next two years the Dyers were out of synch in their beliefs: when Joseph wanted to join the Shakers, Mary did not; then the reverse would be true. Although Mary and Joseph would each later portray how they came to join the Shakers very differently, the fact was the Dyers willingly became Shakers in January 1813. With their five children, Mancer, and several newly converted neighbors, Mary and Joseph moved to Enfield.

At first both seemed quite satisfied with their new life. As was customary with new converts, the Dyer family and their possessions were divided among the three different Shaker "families," subsets of the larger 134-member Enfield Shaker community. Each Shaker family had its own dwelling house, industries, and meeting space. As Shakers, Mary, Joseph, and the children learned to redirect their individual personal ties away from one another and toward the community as a whole. They learned to work for the good of the community, rather than themselves as individuals, and to obey without question the directions and teachings of the elders, the leaders of the hierarchically organized society. But as Joseph grew more and more attached to his new communal family, Mary grew restless. She had not become a religious leader, and in fact her life as a Shaker was just as work-filled, and more restrictive, than her life back at the Dyers' northern New Hampshire farm. Frustrated with her lack of religious progress, missing the close connection to her children, and tired of the endless communal labor, Mary decided that the communal life of Shakerism was not for her.

As a Shaker and a wife, Mary lacked the power simply to leave the community on her own. She arranged a meeting with the Shaker elders and Joseph. The elders were not unhappy with her decision to leave; Mary had been a difficult novitiate, frequently proposing unwelcome amendments to the Shaker faith. And since the Dyers' marriage had been troubled long before they joined the sect, Joseph, too, was unconcerned with his wife's departure. Until, that is, she requested the return of their five children, who then ranged in age from seven to fifteen. Citing the standard and legally binding indenture both Mary and Joseph had signed the previous year, giving custody of the children to the Shakers, the elders refused to release the Dyer children. Joseph agreed with them and claimed he had no right to give Mary the children, nor any duty to provide for her. Mary's stunned anguish turned to stone-cold anger. She threatened to expose the Shakers; the elders warned her she would suffer. Distraught, and convinced she could help her children best by seeking outside support, in January 1815 Mary abandoned Shakerism. She snatched her youngest son and in a frenzied sleigh ride, pursued by a furious Joseph, Mary escaped to the world. Joseph quickly retrieved the child and Mary found herself very much alone.

Mary soon discovered that although she had freed herself from the Shakers, she was still bound to her husband. But without her family around her she was in an ambiguous position. She was a wife, yet apart from her husband, and a mother, yet without the care of her children. There was no social category for a woman estranged from a husband who had joined the Shakers. As a married woman, she was entitled to the protection and support of her husband, who would provide the goods necessary for her survival, including appropriate shelter, clothing, food, and other supplies. Mary in turn would use these to care for the family. She would protect his reputation, and thus that of the entire Dyer family, by acting in an honorable way. This common-law agreement formed the foundation of marriage and of community order and stability. But once Mary left Joseph's residence, even if a Shaker village, she had effectively broken the civil contract between husband and wife. The consequences of this were severe. On February 18, 1815, Joseph alerted local residents and merchants by posting a "runaway wife" notice in the local newspaper, the *Dartmouth Gazette*: "Whereas Mary my lawful wife, has absented herself from my place of residence, and thereby has refused my support and protection. These are therefore to forbid all persons trusting or harboring her on my account. As I shall not consider myself liable to pay any debt of her contracting after this date."[3]

Mary was physically alone, but legally, by the common-law doctrine of coverture, she was united with her husband as one legal entity, effectively one person. But the power of that single entity resided entirely with Joseph, and his advertisement underscored the economic realities for women in the early nineteenth century. As a wife, Mary could not contract a debt on her own, keep wages from her own labor, enter a lawsuit, or sell property. A wife purchased household goods and personal supplies on her husband's, not her own, account. But a runaway wife advertisement circumscribed that economic activity by alerting merchants to refuse a miscreant woman's debts. Without Joseph's assent, Mary had no entree into the economic realm. Socially ambiguous and legally invisible, Mary found herself in dire straits. Perhaps in desperation, or perhaps because she interpreted Joseph's notice as a promise to provide as a husband should, Mary returned to the Shaker village and her husband.

But both set conditions on their reunion: Mary demanded independence, Joseph demanded obedience.

Not surprisingly, a nonbelieving wife living within the Shaker community was disruptive, and shortly after Mary's return Joseph published a second notice, revealing just how disagreeable the situation had become. In this advertisement, published in the *Dartmouth Gazette* on March 21, Joseph described Mary as one who was now only "considered to be [his] wife," an indication of the widening mental, as well as marital, separation between them. Specifying that Mary's mind was "unfriendly toward me and my interests," Joseph announced that his notice was a "permanent warning." As Mary refused to behave as a wife should, he was under no obligation to act as a husband.[4]

Mary's indiscretions included her "gadding about," coming and going as she pleased. She entertained visitors at the Shaker village, including two men from nearby Hanover who brought her writing paper and knowledge of marriage law.[5] Joseph later wrote about a mysterious male visitor secreted in Mary's room who refused to answer Joseph's demands for his name and purpose. He grew "suspicious of their evil designs" and worried that Mary's new friends were "plotting mischief," challenging his role as Mary's husband.[6] Joseph's advertisements were meager threats; he had lost control over his wife.

If the elders had found Mary Dyer undesirable as a troublesome novitiate, they now found her intolerable as a former member. She traveled freely and spoke at area churches, to former Shakers, to whoever would listen, and as she practiced her tale orally, she was crafting a narrative to explain—to herself and to others—her extraordinary experience. With the paper received from her Hanover friends, she began to record her story. The Shakers grew increasingly irritated: while living with them, Mary ignored community practices and mocked community beliefs. In short, she had launched an anti-Shaker campaign from within a Shaker village.

The situation became untenable. The elders informed Joseph in no uncertain terms that Mary was his responsibility. She was, after all, still his wife and not a Shaker. A husband was expected to provide shelter for his wife, but the law did not require that the shelter necessarily be with him, and the elders wanted Mary out of their community. Joseph arranged to board Mary in Orford, thirty miles—fully two days' ride—

from the settlement at Enfield. Although Mary would be staying with her sister and brother-in-law, Betsy and Obadiah Tillotson, she was furious at her forced eviction from her husband's home and the distance it put between her and her children. This was the first of a series of boarding arrangements. When the agreement with the Tillotsons expired, Joseph moved her even further away, hiring her board with "strangers," Mary claimed, in Lancaster, New Hampshire. From 1815 to 1818 Joseph placed her in a succession of homes, moving her about, as she later wrote, at his cruel whim.

Still, Mary was hardly passive during this period. Despite the distance, she would make her way back to Enfield and attempt to see her children. Frequently accompanied by town officials or one of her two attorney brothers-in-law, she managed sporadic, and strained, visits with her children, all of whom were well pleased with their Shaker home. Mary continued to tell her story. In each new location, she gained additional sympathizers and knit together a network of friends, family, and supporters on both sides of the Connecticut River from Hanover, New Hampshire, north to the Canadian border. She gathered affidavits attesting to her husband's abusive treatment, and by examining their dates we can trace her journey north and then back south as she abandons Joseph's arrangements and sets out on her own, relying on her network to provide what her husband would not.

Mary's allies supplied shelter, clothing (a fact Mary threw at her husband to shame him), and a sounding board for her coalescing campaign. She gained the support of James Willis, a local trader from the town of Enfield who boarded Mary and extended credit to her, despite Joseph's published warning. Mary found many disappointed former Shakers who were eager to share their allegations of abuse, destroyed families, or wages forfeited in communal labor. Those who worried about their own friends or relatives who had become Shakers also supported her cause. Mary used her new connections effectively—including her access to a group of Vermont attorneys, two of whom were married to her sisters. These lawyers provided practical advice and helped her draw up a petition to the New Hampshire legislature, asking the state to step in and settle this dispute. In June 1817, having failed repeatedly in face-to-face negotiations with Joseph, Mary borrowed a dress and headed to the state capitol at Concord.

Between 1813 and 1815 Mary Dyer had joined and left the Shakers.

Many had done so before her, and many would follow. Yet Mary was not a typical seceder. Motivated by the loss of her children and the irresolvable position in which she found herself, she became an apostate, someone who leaves a faith and then publicly attacks it. Mary's anti-Shaker campaign began on a small scale, in face-to-face conversations. But her campaign was about to take on a new visibility, carried by print across New England and across the country. It is in this context that her first publication, A Brief Statement, was created.

For two years Mary had struggled to survive and to see her children. Visits to the Shaker village prompted only heated arguments that ended in tears and threats, with no solution to her dilemma. What had started as a private domestic dispute now became the subject of state scrutiny. In June 1817, the New Hampshire legislature considered Mary's petition.[7] In her handwritten request, she told her family's history: how the Shakers had deceived them and destroyed their peaceful and productive marriage, leading Joseph to lose his "natural affection" for his wife, and how she had been forbidden her children. When Mary spoke before the assembled legislature, she reported that while she was living in the Shaker community her health had suffered until she was near death, and that she escaped in order to secure help for her endangered children. Her charismatic presentation captivated the legislature. According to Isaac Hill, editor of the New Hampshire Patriot, a Concord newspaper, Mary found that she was "not wanting in talent," and she quickly gained the sympathy of the public who followed this intriguing tale in the newspapers.[8]

Joseph had his turn to speak as well, and he painted a different picture. Instead of a quiet home, Joseph described a raucous marriage in which his wife refused to yield to his demands and directions. And counter to her claims of Shaker deception, he explained that they both had willingly and happily joined the Shakers. He conceded that her experience there was troubled, but, he testified, Mary's difficulties among the Shakers were not the fault of the faith, but rather of her contrary personality. Her aggressive and stubborn nature made her a poor fit in a communal group dependent on mutual support and obedience. Mary's dilemma, he argued, was of her own making.

The Dyer dispute became the talk of Concord and beyond, as the extensive coverage was reprinted in newspapers throughout New England and as far away as Baltimore, Washington, D.C., and Ohio. It was popular because it tapped into subjects that generated both curiosity and worry. The Shakers were still considered a somewhat mysterious sect, and descriptions of Shaker life and the disruption of the Dyer family raised alarm about a religion that challenged Protestantism, patriarchy, and the sanctity of the reproductive family. At the same time, both Mary's and Joseph's accounts revealed marital tensions and stresses that were all too common in a period of rapid cultural and social change. That this story of marital disintegration was set in a celibate Shaker village only magnified the underlying question: What is a family? Were the celibate Shakers, with their community-wide bonds, a family? Could Mary Dyer, as a single mother, lead a proper family?

The legislature had great sympathy for Mary, but there was little they could do. There was considerable reluctance to meddle in the Shakers' private affairs, especially given the ongoing legislative debate on a state religious toleration act. Mary could request a divorce, but the New Hampshire statutes had no law to deal with the Dyers' unusual situation. Divorce was permitted in cases of incest, impotence, adultery, abandonment, or extreme cruelty. Mary implied the latter two causes in her petition, but it was not a good match with the letter and intent of the law. A subcommittee drafted a bill for a legislative divorce, but the governor, hesitant to create a law benefiting only a single individual, let the bill die on his desk. Mary's petition died with it.[9]

The battle was far from over, however. The following summer, Mary returned to Concord with a new petition. In the intervening year, she had enlarged her network, refined her argument, and recast her story from the tale of one wronged wife to a narrative in which she was but one of a number of similarly abused women. She tried new strategies to secure her husband's financial support. She prompted James Willis to sue Joseph in an attempt to force him to pay the debts she had incurred with Willis. The suit failed on appeal when the Shakers produced copies of Joseph's newspaper notice with its "permanent warning."[10] Mary established herself as a resident of the town of Enfield and applied to the selectmen for help. In a contentious meeting between Joseph, Mary, Shaker leaders, town selectmen, and a group of Mary's female supporters, Mary demanded that something be done to provide her with support. Joseph offered only two options: he would support her at his Shaker home, or he would offer an acquittance for life—basically a permanent marital separation. He would give her some of their remaining uncleared land in northern New Hampshire in exchange for her promise not to demand anything else from him. Although this arrangement would provide her with a source of support, acquittances offered little protection to wives. The Dyers would still be married, and thus Mary would be unable to remarry, and she could not sell the property without Joseph's consent. Acquittances were legally unenforceable; if Joseph later changed his mind, Mary would have no recourse. And in a practical sense, wild land was useless to a nearly forty-year-old woman without a husband or children. The meeting ended without a resolution.

Then, in May 1818, Mary forcibly pressed her demands for her children. With the assistance of James Willis and other local supporters, she raised a mob against the Enfield Shakers. The Dyers were not the only couple whose marriage Shakerism disrupted, and Mary had with her a powerful ally, Eunice Hawley Chapman, whose story in New York State mirrored Mary's experience in New Hampshire. Together Eunice and Mary would bring conflict and disorder to both the Enfield Shakers and the surrounding town.

Eunice and James Chapman were married in New York State in 1804. At first their marriage appeared happy, but by 1811 James had grown disillusioned, and he abandoned his family to find work and a new life. In 1813, he joined the Watervliet, New York, Shakers, and thinking he had found salvation, decided to bring his three children and, if she was willing, his wife, to the sect. But Eunice was unwilling. Fearing his children were headed for poverty under Eunice's inadequate care, in October 1814 James surreptitiously slipped back to his former home and stole away the couple's children while Eunice was out on an errand. When she discovered what James had done, Eunice followed him to Watervliet, near Albany, to retrieve her children. Unsuccessful in gaining the children, in 1815 Eunice repeatedly traveled to the Shaker enclave only to argue vociferously with James. She sent threatening letters to the Shaker leaders at New Lebanon, New York, the seat of Shaker power. When direct confrontation and threats failed to resolve the Chapmans' dispute, Eunice brought her quest to a public forum.

In 1817, after two years of unsuccessful efforts to get her children back, Eunice published *An Account of the Shakers*, designed to solicit public awareness of her cause, raise money for her support, and turn public sympathy to her side.[11] With the help of her brother (a New York state legislator), Eunice petitioned the legislature for a divorce. She recounted in vivid detail how her children had been abducted in the cold, upstate New York winter and dragged unwillingly away from their loving mother. Evoking the Indian captivity narrative, she declared that "those who have had their friends taken captive by the savages can better realize my feelings than I can describe!"[12] But here the agents of misery are not Native Americans; the villain is her own husband. Instead of protecting the family, James broke it apart. Instead of raising good citizens, he placed his children in harm's way: "The dear little captives must have almost perished with cold and hunger!"[13] Eunice portrayed James as abandoning his family, selling off the property, and failing to provide food, clothing, or housing. He even took the last sheep. Left without means and without her children, Eunice found herself alone in Albany, wandering the streets in search of work. She had no desire to have her husband return; she claimed that James was intemperate and was abusive and dangerous when drunk. She also claimed to have "ocular" evidence of his adulterous behavior. When some Shaker women accused Eunice of lusting after her own husband, she offered, "If you give me my children, you are welcome to my husband!"[14] To demonstrate her own respectability as a kind woman, capable housekeeper, and good nurse, Eunice included in her text affidavits testifying to her proper standing and James's abysmal behavior.

James responded with an open letter to the state legislature, published in the Albany newspaper (and later printed in papers across New England, including in Concord, New Hampshire, the very week Mary Dyer's 1817 petition appeared before the legislature there). In his account of their marriage, James reported that he thought Eunice was a nice girl until shortly after their marriage, when he learned her "natural temper and disposition." By "sad experience" he found that her personality was "a fatal bar to social union and happiness in the conjugal state."[15] He stated that he did not want to harm his wife, but that the "imperious necessity" of preventing further slander on the innocent Shakers forced him to "make an open declaration of facts which, but for her own folly, might have been buried in oblivion."[16] Buried in oblivion:

had Eunice kept quiet, her faults would have been invisible outside the family. But since she had broken marital expectations by stepping into a public light, James reasoned, the invisible was now fair game. Continuing his accusations, he claimed that Eunice was excommunicated from her church because of the "fatal effects of her calumniating tongue,"[17] and that she verbally abused him and stole part of his estate. He admitted to drinking—"the unhappy and too frequent consequence of domestic troubles"—and said he had gone to the Shakers as his cure.[18] His decision to leave her is instructively worded: "I resolved to separate myself from a woman who, instead of seeking my happiness and soothing my grief, seemed bent on destroying the one and adding fresh pangs to the other."[19] Eunice believed James was to provide for her needs; James wanted Eunice to make him happy. Each had failed the other.

By May of 1818 both women were desperate. Mary Dyer had failed to secure Joseph's support or the return of any of her children. Eunice Chapman had received a legislative divorce in New York State, but her children and former husband had disappeared. Traveling in secret, Eunice came to Enfield, where she had learned her children had been hidden. Together, she and Mary planned their attack, and with a group of supporters they headed to the Shaker village.

The mob event lasted five days and waxed and waned in its intensity. By day Eunice and Mary traveled to the Shaker enclave and demanded to see their children. Sometimes local officials accompanied them; at other times one of the women would appear alone, or with just a few neighboring women. By night, townspeople worked to keep the Shakers on edge by firing guns and patrolling the borders of the Shaker settlement on horseback. By the fourth evening the tension had reached a peak, and a large crowd gathered at the village. Without a divorce or custody agreement, Mary effectively had no claim to her children, and the mob ceased to back her. But Eunice rallied the assemblage to her defense, and after failing to reach an agreement with James in a protracted and noisy argument, she and the mob ransacked the village. They stopped only when the Chapmans' young son, George, was discovered hiding in a barn. Eunice quickly whisked the unwilling boy away. A year later she would return with a writ of habeas corpus and retrieve, peacefully, her two daughters.[20]

Once again Mary Dyer was left without satisfaction, and the mob attack had left bitter feelings toward her among the Enfield townspeople. In late May 1818, forty-seven male residents of Enfield filed a petition asking the legislature to step in and prevent such uproars. They complained that the Shaker rearrangement of the family left nonbelieving women to wander the streets "crying" and disrupting community peace and quiet. Although Mary cited this petition as evidence of support on her behalf, the underlying motive was the residents' fear that they would bear financial responsibility when husbands joined the Shakers and abandoned their wives.[21]

Still without financial resources and bolstered by what she interpreted as community support, Mary placed a second petition before the legislature in June 1818.[22] This time she borrowed a strategy common among petitioners, one she may have learned from Eunice Chapman: she printed her complaints in a small pamphlet and distributed the text to each legislator in advance of her hearing. Learning of the work, the public's curiosity was once again raised, and Joseph Spear, a Concord printer, wasted no time in making it available for mass consumption at a low price. Once again Mary, Joseph, their marriage, and the Shakers were the talk of Concord.[23]

With a printed text, the public could read even more details of the Dyers' marriage and ponder Mary's allegations. *A Brief Statement of the Sufferings of Mary Dyer, Occasioned by the Shakers* included a revised narrative that made the Shakers the centerpiece of the drama. Mary included affidavits and certificates that testified to her good standing and to additional Shaker evils. An extract from the Shakers' *Testimony of Christ's Second Appearing* attempted to use the sect's own words against them. She concluded the new work with her 1818 legislative petition, the petition of the Enfield residents, and an open letter denying she sought a divorce, only the return of her children. Since legislators had worried about enacting a law solely for her benefit, Mary sought to demonstrate that Shaker abuse affected many women, children, and the local communities that had to endure their distress. She also responded to the critics who asked why she had joined the Shakers in the first place. Here she emphasized that her enrollment had been temporary and that she had been deluded by Shaker lies. Once she realized the errors of the Shakers' ways, she fought to extricate herself and her children.

Once again the legislative hearings became fodder for public gossip. The legislature appointed a special committee to travel to the Canterbury Shaker community, just outside Concord, to conduct an investigation into Mary Dyer's claims. Despite the gross invasion of privacy such an investigation necessitated, the Shakers willingly allowed the legislators and committee members to interview the sisters and brothers, including about such topics as the women's menstrual habits, in response to Mary's claims that the Shakers were not, in fact, celibate and used some sort of medicine to make women infertile and thus able to have sex without consequence.

The investigating committee found nothing amiss at the Shaker village and instead praised the Shakers' industry, as well as the polite, hardworking children they encountered. While not supportive of the practices of celibacy and alternative family structure—which they found ill-conceived—the committee declared the Shakers to be models of good citizenship. Mary was given leave to withdraw her petition.

Despite the setback, Mary did have some success in 1818. Her *Brief Statement* had demonstrated the power of print to gain sympathy and disseminate information. The newspaper coverage and two editions of her pamphlet carried her story across New England and beyond. Abram Van Vleet, an Ohio anti-Shaker and a newspaper editor, learned of Chapman's and Dyer's attempts to retrieve their children. Van Vleet produced *An Account of the Conduct of the Shakers*, which included an edited version of Eunice Chapman's second pamphlet, a report on the Enfield mob, and a lengthy deposition from Mary Dyer. The book effectively carried the women's complaints to the western arena of anti-Shaker activity, enlarging their sphere of recognition and potential support. The distribution of her story through the newspaper, her own pamphlet, and extracts contained in the publications of Chapman and Van Vleet established Mary Dyer as the symbol of anti-Shaker activity—to the anti-Shakers, a symbol of Shaker cruelty; to Shaker supporters, the epitome of vindictiveness.

The Shakers were taken aback by this unexpected turn of events. The publication and popularity of *A Brief Statement* had caught them by surprise, and they could rush into print only a "remonstrance," the short document initially drawn up for the legislature as a rebuttal to Mary's 1818 legislative petition.[24] As Mary's fame spread, with a second edition of *A Brief Statement* published in Boston, Joseph Dyer felt compelled to respond in kind. In February 1819 he published *A Compendious Narrative, Elucidating the Character, Disposition and Conduct of Mary Dyer*, with rival publishers now working together to entice readers. Joseph professed a hesitation to enter such a public debate, since he had "ever considered a contest between a man and his wife the most disagreeable and shameful of all contests." Yet, because Mary had "imposed upon" innocent readers, he felt it his duty to counter her accusations.[25] Now readers had two sides of the story to consider. The inviting texts challenged readers: read and decide.

A Brief Statement and *A Compendious Narrative* let us hear two perspectives on the same story of family dissolution. The narratives address a public audience, a court of public opinion, while they also speak to each other. This type of discourse presented a new way of arguing, and a new opportunity for learning about the power, and danger, of print.

The Dyers' narratives can be read in the context of several genres of popular literature. They are at first glance personal narratives. As the historian Ann Fabian notes, inexpensive paper and low printing costs allowed anyone with literacy, a little money, and a story to tell to tell it in print. Fabian describes a plethora of publications in which authors turned their strange circumstances into financial gain. Prisoners of war, pirate captives, criminals, and beggars all told their unusual tales.[26] Likewise, Mary and Joseph Dyer were able to capitalize on the events that had gained their names, briefly, household recognition. For Mary, her publications would literally be a source of income and identity. For Joseph, publishing his rebuttal provided a public stage on which to defend himself and the Shakers from his wife's accusations. Mary published to solicit the support of the public, whom she invited to become actively involved in her life. Joseph wrote to keep the public out of his private affairs, railing against the intrusion of outsiders into decisions that were his alone to make. Both authors explained and justified the events of their lives, weaving them into a larger story about the difficulties of being a wife or husband in the early republic.

Taken together, the Dyers' accounts share characteristics of divorce-trial narratives, paired publications in which adversarial parties laid bare their dispute. While contemporary marriages can dissolve without "fault," in early-nineteenth-century divorce cases one party would be declared innocent and the other to blame. When the Dyers wrote their pamphlets they were not in divorce proceedings, but they were both trying to reorganize their family situation. Divorce was one option, although, as we have seen, a difficult one for the Dyers to achieve. Nonetheless, both Dyers used conventions of the divorce-trial narrative to make their cases. Each asserts the other broke the marital contract and failed to be a dutiful spouse, and each accused the other of sexual impropriety or deviance, the surefire way of proving spousal guilt. Although Mary revealed Joseph's susceptibility to Shaker seduction in A Brief Statement, the majority of the text is about her experiences at the Shaker village, where for Mary her troubles commenced, and the period after she left. Joseph, on the other hand, provided more details of their life before the move to Enfield, focusing on the faults and characteristics that made Mary an irresponsible and flawed wife with or without Shakerism. Intriguing and personal, divorce narratives allowed readers to enter vicariously someone else's marriage while simultaneously reflecting on their own behavior as husband or wife.

A Brief Statement is also an anti-Shaker narrative. Since 1780, shortly after the Shakers began openly proselytizing, disappointed former converts had taken pen in hand to seek revenge, to reestablish themselves in their communities, and to warn others to avoid their fate. Between 1780 and 1860 some two dozen pamphlets were published by apostate Shakers. These texts provide important insiders' accounts of Shakerism from those whom the faith failed to satisfy. Mary Dyer was the only female apostate to publish, and her accounts, five major publications from 1817 to 1852, are unique for two reasons. First, she provides a rare female anti-Shaker perspective on life within a Shaker community. Mary's texts record the work, leadership, and experiences of Shaker women, a perspective not easily available to male apostate authors in the gender-segregated Shaker community. Second, Shakers and her Shaker husband refuted her publications with several works of their own, something that did not happen with male apostate authors, whose written works, for the most part, went unchallenged. The intense public interest in and forceful Shaker response to Mary's allegations gave her works a potency that few other anti-Shaker works generated.

Anti-Shaker activists used mobs, legal wrangling in the courts, and legislative petitions in their efforts to eradicate Shakerism, but books were among the most effective weapons in the anti-Shaker arsenal. A minister named Valentine Rathbun published the first account in 1781. In *An Account of the Matter, Form, and Manner of a New and Strange Religion* he recounted that the pleasing words of elders seduced him and, at Rathbun's urging, most of his congregation into the faith, but once converted he learned a new side to Shakerism, which he now saw as nothing short of a delusion. He warned fellow ministers to guard their congregations lest the Shakers destroy their churches as they had his.[27]

Other writers followed. Amos Taylor (1782) argued that the Shakers threatened American independence; Benjamin West (1783) drew on centuries of anti-Catholic fervor to allege that the Shakers were a tool of the Roman Pope. Daniel Rathbun (Valentine's brother) wrote an account of how his family was destroyed by Shakerism (1795), and Reuben Rathbun (Valentine's son) complained about the elders' hold on positions of power, effectively blocking Reuben, and others, from leadership roles (1800). Most anti-Shaker authors, these included, touched on multiple issues as they made their argument. Not all of the anti-Shaker literature was produced by former Shakers; some writers had never joined the sect but voiced a variety of complaints nonetheless. James Smith in Ohio wrote about the destruction of his son's family on behalf of his daughter-in-law (1810).[28] Many other authors challenged the Shakers' theological views, especially after 1808, when the Shakers themselves entered print culture with the publication of *The Testimony of Christ's Second Appearing*.[29] Several Protestant ministers, for example, wrote tracts examining the Shakers' claims in minute detail, and offered rebuttals bristling with Biblical citations to refute their theology.[30]

In the second decade of the nineteenth century, Thomas Brown added his voice to the anti-Shaker chorus with a dramatic narrative of falling into and out of Shakerism. Pamphlets and books played a central role in his story. Brown had read Valentine Rathbun's account and wanted to see the Shakers for himself. He joined but later was seduced away by rereading Rathbun and seeing his allegations in a new light.[31] Printed matter by anti-Shaker or Shaker hands was a double-edged sword: as easily as it could lead one into the faith, it could just as easily lead one out. The Shakers learned quickly how problematic anti-Shaker texts could be. One exasperated elder lamented the challenges of gaining new converts when anti-Shaker texts presented such "stumbling blocks."[32]

Print could travel great distances, introduce Shakerism to people who had never seen a Shaker village, and continue to speak beyond the life of the author. By the 1820s, when Mary Dyer began her writing career, literacy in the United States was expanding rapidly. The production of printed material was now easier and cheaper, and growing transportation networks allowed it to be distributed faster and farther. More than a dozen authors had written numerous tracts against the Shakers by 1820; another two dozen tracts would be added in the next three decades. And during the 1820s and beyond, new venues for information about Shakerism emerged: magazines and newspapers published the accounts of visitors to Shaker villages; fiction with Shaker themes (including romance) became popular, and the Shakers themselves published a wide range of pamphlets, books, and tracts, as they had quickly learned the strategic advantages of appearing in public in print.[33]

As an anti-Shaker narrative, Mary Dyer's *Brief Statement* shared conventions of the genre Valentine Rathbun had inaugurated in 1780, drawing on such tropes as the hypocritical elders hiding a secret, unspecified abuse, and the elders' mysterious power to delude believers. Yet Mary's account is unusual in that it is written from a woman's perspective. The only female apostate to publish extensively against the Shakers, Mary offered a unique addition to the corpus of apostate literature. Both Mary's account and that of Eunice Chapman, an anti-Shaker though not apostate author, revealed the gender limitations of their day.[34]

Mary Dyer modeled her story on a well-known genre, the Indian captivity narrative, tales of trial and suffering at the hands of savages and ultimate redemption by the grace of God. In her vivid rendition, she is captive first to a husband who takes her away to the Shakers, and then to the Shaker leaders who are unmoved by a mother's agony. Mary also drew on sentiment as a way to gain public support, painting scenes of women crying as their children were taken away by the Shakers and Mary's own tears rendering her unable to write. Sentiment was designed to move people, specifically men, to action. Like many anti-Shaker writers, Mary painted the Shakers as an "Other," a group not aligned with American values and traditions but rather styled as Catholics, Masons, foreigners, or "savages." Mary used the Shakers as a convenient foil, one that would make it clear why her children should be returned to her. Such a dangerous environment, a Shaker village of celibate women, could only produce the most drastic of effects on young, tender, malleable minds. Mary insisted that her children arrived at the Enfield settlement under the agency of their father, who even before coming under the influence of Shakerism was a poor husband.

The title page of *A Brief Statement* reflected Mary's isolation. The tract is "written by herself," a claim to the authenticity of her tale but also to the state of her sad, lonely life. Here was a woman who was married, yet alone, and the title page points out who is to blame. Her "sufferings" were "occasioned by the Society called Shakers." "Affidavits and certificates" were appended to her text, testifying to her reputation as a dedicated wife and loving mother, a woman who was faithful, truthful, economical, and hard-working. Her deponents supported her version of events, implied that Joseph had broken many promises, and attacked the Shakers for a variety of misconduct.

Joseph countered with a husband's narrative. It is instructive that he writes not as a Shaker per se, but, as his title page proclaims, "her husband," clearly marking the authoritative base on which he grounds his argument. Two points serve as the basis for his case: that he is the rightful head of the family "by the laws of God [and] the Creator,"[35] and that Mary is an unfit mother and a disreputable wife. Mary writes of her children's promise thwarted by Shakerism; Joseph calls the children "peevish and cross"[36] and faults Mary's child-rearing skills. Mary alleges that Shakers harm children with hard work and little rest; Joseph describes Mary punishing a child with a severe whipping. Mary hints that a Shaker elder had been selected to be her illicit partner; Joseph alleges that Mary was unfaithful. Mary asserts that Shaker celibacy is unnatural; Joseph counters that his wife made their marriage celibate long before they learned of Shakerism.

Like Mary, Joseph included affidavits from former Stewartstown neighbors, from family, and from Shakers, affirming that he was a kind man and Mary an obsessive woman who preferred to lead rather than be led. Further, they testified that it was Mary who was the more eager of the two to join the Shakers. Two affidavits were particularly devastating: statements from the two oldest Dyer children, who wrote that they were satisfied with their life in the Shaker village.

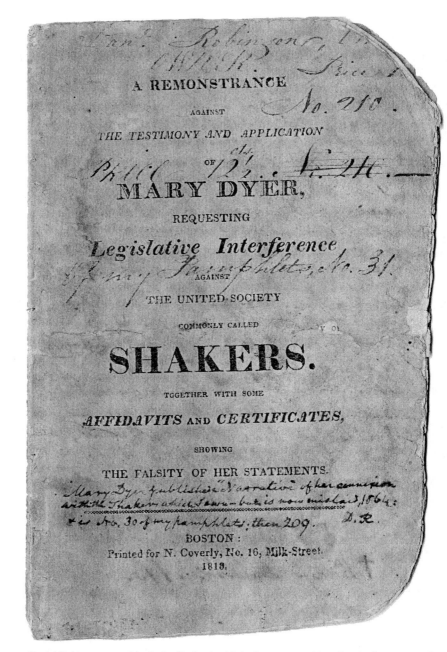

A REMONSTRANCE

AGAINST

THE TESTIMONY AND APPLICATION

OF

MARY DYER,

REQUESTING

Legislative Interference

AGAINST

THE UNITED SOCIETY

COMMONLY CALLED

SHAKERS.

TOGETHER WITH SOME

AFFIDAVITS AND CERTIFICATES,

SHOWING

THE FALSITY OF HER STATEMENTS.

BOSTON :
Printed for N. Coverly, No. 16, Milk-Street.
1818.

Daniel Robinson owned both the Shakers' published response to Mary Dyer's allegations and, as his manuscript note indicated, Mary Dyer's *A Brief Statement*. As publishers had encouraged, the public read both sides.

Mary Dyer! be on thy guard;—
All thoughts of peace discard;
Thy foes press on thee hard;
Nought will their steps retard,
  Till thou art overcome:
Summon all thy winter friends,
And Truth, who best of all defends
The cause where Innocence attends,
And who to the Oppressed lends
  A voice whene'er they're dumb +

Tell them—the Shakers, men of peace,
.... their Order may decrease
...... "Brief Statement" ne'er will cease
To persecute thee, or to fleece
  Those men whose wealth they grasp:
Bid them step forth to aid thy cause,
Nor longer hear thy wrongs & pause,
But try the influence of the Laws,
To snatch thee from those harpies' claws
  Ere drawn is thy last gasp!

                                    D. R.

† Witness Balaam's Ass.

Daniel Robinson penned this rhyming warning to Mary Dyer on the inside cover of his copy of the *Remonstrance*.

Publishers had urged readers to consider both accounts, and Joseph's text made it easy for readers to compare the two tracts. Just as Mary provided page numbers for specific passages in *The Testimony of Christ's Second Appearing*, Joseph cites specific page numbers from Mary's account when making his counter-allegations. Two extant copies of the Shakers' remonstrance against Mary Dyer's testimony indicate that readers did compare texts. In one copy, a man named Daniel Robinson recorded on the title page that he owned both Joseph's and Mary's narratives, and on the following page wrote a lengthy poem in which he warned Mary to "be on thy guard!" Another individual, name unknown, recorded on his copy that Mary had not proved that the Shakers were despotic.[37] Letters dating from this period indicate that readers shared copies of the texts with friends and that some people, after reading one or the other account, were eager to visit the Shakers and see the sect for themselves.[38]

Interestingly, despite Mary's pleas for her children, the five Dyer offspring are little discussed in either account.[39] Joseph offers several examples of Mary's poor skills and lack of interest in child-rearing and complains that he was often forced into the maternal role. Mary says little about Joseph's relationship with the children and instead focuses on the Shakers, to whom the children now belonged. The battle in print centered on the character and behavior of the child-rearer, just as would be the case in a custody dispute in a court of law.

The paired publications of Mary and Joseph Dyer made good reading, but what was the solution to this troubled marriage? To simply let unhappy wives out of their marriages was problematic. Divorced women, released from their marriage bonds and out from under the protection of husbands, were potentially, as the historian Norma Basch notes, "loose women," with the moral associations that accompany that term today.[40] While another Shaker apostate author, Absolem Blackburn, styled himself a "modern pamphleteer" for the ease with which he could spout his views in print, for Mary print was a more treacherous ally.[41] Although there was sympathy for her plight, the sympathy ended when Mary stopped sobbing and started speaking in front of the legislature. Eunice Chapman was lampooned in a satirical play and lambasted in the press, with headlines across the country alerting readers with exasperation to "another Eunice Chapman story."[42] When Mary appeared before the New Hampshire legislature she was suspected of having a hidden agenda; she was praised for "talent, confidence, and enthusiasm," but the praise was colored by doubt as to "the sincerity of her motives."[43] Especially for Mary, who had once lived as a Shaker, the public had a hard time reconciling her pleas to be a private mother with her very public activities.

And the public was equally hesitant to let men out of their marriage vows. The New York legislature feared that granting the Chapmans a divorce would start a flood of men running to the Shakers to escape marital responsibility. Townspeople living near Shaker enclaves did not welcome divorce-by-Shakerism. When Eunice Chapman and Mary Dyer combined forces in the ill-advised mob against the Enfield Shakers, the Shakers responded that "it was a pity that the United States were so reduced as to be stirred up by two old women running in the streets."[44] In 1828 the residents of Enfield again sought legislative help against the Shakers, who had continued to make women noisy. When Stephen Folsom joined the Enfield Shakers, his wife ran away and hid her household goods and children, fearing that she too would be forced to join. The marital dispute prompted three new petitions to the legislature, in total signed by nearly two hundred residents of the town of Enfield. Once again the legislature refused to interfere. Folsom railed against local interference in a newspaper advertisement addressed to "meddlesome neighbors" who intruded into his private dilemma.[45] And as had happened with Mary Dyer, the Shakers denied responsibility for the women and passed that job on to the husbands. In *The Other Side of the Question*, written in 1818, Richard McNemar, a Shaker, insisted that the Dyers' and similar marital conflicts were merely "domestic broils" and not of Shaker doing, or for Shaker solving.[46] As had happened to Mary many times before, although *A Brief Statement* garnered immense public interest, debate and scrutiny, it came to nothing practical. She was still married, still without her children, and still in desperation.

After her second failed legislative hearing, one of the legislators told Mary Dyer that if she had more evidence of the Shakers' abuse of women, there might be something that could be done. Mary set off across New Hampshire gathering affidavits and writing her magnum opus, *A*

Portraiture of Shakerism, a four-hundred-page book detailing the full extent of Shakerism's evils. The print battle continued: after *A Portraiture of Shakerism* was published in 1823, the Shakers rebutted her claims in *A Review of Portraiture* (1824), to which she replied in print with *A Reply to a Review* (1824).[47] Some of the same deponents from *A Brief Statement* and *A Compendious Narrative* reappeared in these latest pamphlets. Collectively, Mary Dyer's publications show that her experience in the hierarchal group was no more than her marital woes writ large. She complained that she had no input into decisions and little autonomy, and that she was constrained by endless labor and duties. Although she was relieved of the individual care of her children, she was required to perform communal labor to help support the Shaker village, whose members numbered almost 150. Mary sought autonomy and independence; she could not find it with her husband, nor with the Shakers. Throughout the 1820s she traveled New England, lecturing and selling her books, and while some agreed with her perceptions of the dangers of Shakerism, others found her writings nothing more than "horrid lies."[48] As the Shakers continued to build neat villages and develop productive agricultural endeavors, the reading public increasingly favored the Shakers and dismissed Mary's claims.[49]

In the 1820s the New Hampshire legislature, having pondered the Dyers' situation for several years, carefully amended the state's divorce law, permitting divorce in situations where a spouse joined a sect that negates the marital bond. With this new statute in place, Mary filed for divorce in 1828. The divorce was contested, but in 1830 the courts granted Mary her divorce. She returned to her maiden name, bought a house, and settled into a solitary life a few miles from the Shaker village where four of her five children would live for the rest of their lives. Two decades later and well into her seventies, she was still campaigning to prevent her sad predicament from happening to other women. In 1847 she published *The Rise and Progress of the Serpent*, an abridged version of *A Portraiture of Shakerism*.[50] Mary and her still considerable allies used this work to stir up public support in advance of a massive petition to the New Hampshire legislature. With over four hundred signatures, the 1848 petition once again requested that the state step in to circumscribe Shaker affairs. The petitioners were unsuccessful. Undeterred, Mary published her final work, *Shakerism Exposed*, in 1852, and she continued her anti-Shaker campaign until her death in 1867.[51] Joseph produced a second edition of *A Compendious Narrative* in 1826 to battle Mary's continued accusations, and it was still being used in the 1840s as the counterpoint to her tracts. Joseph remained a Shaker for the remainder of his life. He died at the age of eighty-five in 1858.

Mary had turned the misfortune of a Shaker husband into a commodity and offered several lessons for her readers. They learned that Mary's independence was hard won. Although she thrived as an advocate for the cause of injured women, in reality she needed men to do so. Male friends and family worked in politics or the legal system, and these educated men had connections, money, and knowledge that assisted her in placing petitions before the legislature. Her readers learned from her experience that if their husbands would not help them, they had to turn to other men, and in particular to the legislature, to act in their place and to help them out of their legal and social limbos. They learned that without men, wives had insignificant public roles, little power, and few chances to be heard. But they also learned that they had a story to tell, and that print was a powerful medium in which to tell it. And women who read Mary's story learned the dangers of straying too far from the normative ideal: a woman who led mobs, spoke before the legislature, and sold books in public may have gained some public sympathy, but she was hardly the model mother society prized.

Joseph and his readers learned of the potential for the dangerous intrusion of others into the marital sphere. Joseph railed against the meddling of outsiders, asserting that he still had control of the family whether he and his wife lived with the Shakers or did not. As much as Mary's pamphlets and activities were novel, her message was one of tradition: a male headed his household, caring for his family and providing his wife with what she needed. And as radical as the Shakers appeared, their message was the same. In refusing to get involved in domestic broils, they asserted the husband's role as supreme, and they recognized the traditional family unit, even when they themselves chose to alter it.

Print spread Mary Dyer's message across towns, the state, and eventually across the country. As a narrative of a bad marriage and as an anti-Shaker text, *A Brief Statement* was a commodity and offered ideas for eager readers to debate in the court of public opinion. But as the debate moved back and forth between supporting or condemning the wife, public opinion could not deny the fundamental truth of the husband's text: as part of the defense of his way of life, both as a Shaker *and* as a husband, Joseph's text asserted the primacy of patriarchy, in families both celibate and not.

In the spring of 1819, following the failure of James Willis's lawsuit, Joseph Dyer offered Mary her own home near her children. Although her friends warned her of deception, Mary returned once again to the Shaker village hoping that this time Joseph would abide by his promise to provide for his wife in a suitable manner. But once there, Mary learned she had been deceived. There was no separate house for her; she was to live in a solitary room in the midst of the Shaker enclave. Once again confined among the Shakers, her health declined and she feared she would die. Mary later described how she escaped this third "captivity" by pulling the nails from a door and running away in the dark night. Before she next attempted to see her children, like a pilot about to make a dangerous flight, she made her itinerary known and left her desperate note in Mills Olcott's kitchen.

Mary Dyer moved from Olcott's kitchen to a very public stage. Throughout the 1820s and the following decades newspapers, pamphlets, broadsides and books kept her story alive. In her later works she would borrow themes from the temperance and abolition movements and the new science of electricity to merge her argument with current social concerns. One theme remained constant: the power of men to control women's lives. As Mary poignantly asked in *A Brief Statement*: "Who can have sensations with me? Oh! Can any? I think some mothers can, but they cannot relieve me. I call for the tender feelings of fathers to have pity on the feminine sex."[52]

Mary's obituary noted that she had "a masculine cast of mind and thought and acted with great independence."[53] Later authors would describe her even less kindly. One can see her as a desperate mother or a shrill opportunist, as a woman with a religious calling or a self-centered zealot. Was Joseph a cruel cad or a reticent man overwhelmed by a strong-willed wife? Did he find salvation with the Shakers or a convenient escape from his troubled marriage? Or both? When Mary's and Joseph's lives intersected with Shakerism, the War of 1812 loomed, the economy was unstable, and New England farming was becoming increasingly difficult.

New ideas about marriage, the roles of women, and the nature of children challenged older assumptions. Life was changing, and fast. Together, *A Brief Statement* and *A Compendious Narrative* reveal the multiple challenges for men, women, and sectarian religion in the early nineteenth century. Take away the rural farmhouse and put the Dyers in a suburban housing development; replace the couple's joint desires for preaching with a two-career household. Instead of the Shakers, imagine a family joining a commune or any of the many alternative religious groups that continue to dot the American landscape. The Dyers asked readers to decide what constituted a family, and what responsibilities and obligations husbands and wives had to one another in circumstances both good and bad. We continue to ask those very same questions today.

A

BRIEF STATEMENT

OF THE

SUFFERINGS

OF

MARY DYER,

OCCASIONED BY THE SOCIETY CALLED

SHAKERS.

WRITTEN BY HERSELF.

TO WHICH IS ADDED,

AFFIDAVITS AND CERTIFICATES;

ALSO,

A DECLARATION FROM THEIR OWN PUBLICATION.

[COPY RIGHT SECURED.]

BOSTON :

PUBLISHED BY WILLIAM S. SPEAR.

1818.

A

BRIEF STATEMENT

OF THE

SUFFERINGS

OF

MARY DYER,

OCCASIONED BY THE SOCIETY CALLED

SHAKERS.

WRITTEN BY HERSELF.

TO WHICH IS ADDED,

AFFIDAVITS AND CERTIFICATES;

ALSO,

A DECLARATION FROM THEIR OWN PUBLICATION.

[COPY RIGHT SECURED.]

BOSTON:

PUBLISHED BY WILLIAM S. SPEAR.

1818.

To the Honorable the Senate, and House of Representatives of the State of New Hampshire, in General Court convened—The great confidence I repose in your candor and wisdom, causes me to lay before you my situation; earnestly entreating you, by all the affections of a mother, that I may again be restored to my long lost children. This I humbly pray.

Mary Dyer,
Enfield, June 6, 1818.[1]

⌒⌒

A BRIEF STATEMENT, &C.

I, MARY DYER, was lawfully married to Joseph Dyer, in the year 1799; We resided in Stewartstown, in the county of Coos, and State of New-Hampshire. We lived quietly together eleven years, though there had been some disagreeables by my husband's being unsteady, and given sometimes to intoxication. We had five children, and were in good circumstances. We were united in a hope of salvation, through Christ. We were of the Baptist profession; yet as there was no church established we stood single characters. The people thought it expedient there should be a church established in those parts. Accordingly, in June 1811, the people assisted the preacher to go to the State of New-York, to move his family among us. When he returned, instead of bringing his family, he brought some Shaker books, and a recommendation from the Shakers in the State of New-York, to those in Enfield, in New-Hampshire, and said he had joined the Shaker's society.[2] This was astonishing and disappointing; and the first information I ever had of the Shakers. Strange as it was, Mr. Dyer was induced to go and see them. I had strong impressions that their belief was contrary to the gospel. Mr. Dyer was anxious I should go with him to make the Shaker's a visit. In July we went—Mr. Dyer was pleased with them at the first sight, and said he wanted no farther evidence to convince him they were right. It caused me grief to see him so enraptured with new imaginations. Mr. Dyer joined them, intending to set up a society in Stewartstown. We returned after a tedious visit. I could not believe with him, and it was distressing to have that union broke which we had hitherto supported. I endeavored to convince him of their errors by Scripture—(I believed him to be pious,) my reasoning appeared in vain. He said, unless I would be a Shaker he would carry the children to the Shakers and leave me. My sorrow was great—It was the first time I ever knew him discontented with me. I offered to live with him as a slave if he would let me live with my children; but no. Oh! the sorrow at the thought of being separated from my family.[3] I endeavoured to reason with him again. I observed, in case I should go I could not have his care and protection, unless the Elders[4] should see proper, and perhaps be separated from my children; and if I was not contented to stay, my friends would reject me on the account of going to the Shakers; and I should be left destitute without protection, and childless, without home or friends.

My grief was almost insupportable. He made this reply: In case I would go he would ever provide for and protect me. I should have the care of my children; and in case either of us was discontented, he would have three children, and I should have two. To this he called God to witness. This removed my fears. Then I strove to gain every favorable idea of the Shakers: so that in case I should go I might be contented. After I began to gain so many favorable ideas of them, I observed I thought they might be right. When Mr. Dyer learnt that there was a possibility of my believing in them, and my mind gathered towards them, he appeared displeased. He left reading the Shaker's Bible. Immediately, he turned against me and said I should go out of his family, if I did not renounce my belief in the Shakers. He threatened me severely: I told him I was willing to comply with any thing that was reasonable; but he was so changeable that I could place no dependance on him.

In the month of August, we mutually gave up the idea of being Shakers, and became harmonious. In February, 1812, he went to Portsmouth, N.H. and he called on the Shakers in Alfred, and returned home strong in the belief that the Shakers were the only true Church.[5] We wrote them a friendly letter, as though they were Christians.

After war was proclaimed between America and Great Britain,[6] as we lived near Canada, Mr. Dyer was anxious to have his family secluded among the Shakers. In autumn, as he went to visit his friends in Connecticut,[7] he took my only daughter, who was then eleven, and my son Orville, who was eight years old, to leave with the Shakers at Enfield, to see how they would like, until he returned—he said perhaps for four or six weeks. When he returned, he had left them there and brought orders from the Shaker Elders for me to go there immediately with my other children, and they would provide for us a house and other necessaries to make the family comfortable. I was unwilling to go without my husband; and I had a promise from him, that if I was dissatisfied with the situation, I might fetch my children back. To this he consented.

After a tedious journey, I arrived at Enfield, with my children, January 1st, 1813. I was glad to find my absent children. My little son Orville was sick, though not confined. He was anxious for my care, and desired to return with me. I expected no other but his return, as I did not find any house prepared for me, and everything was disagreeable. They would not let me have the child, and said, as his father had left him, I should not take him. A brother, older, was so grieved for his younger brother, that he offered to stay in his stead—But no.[8] I then asked for the outside garments of the other children, to return with me to their father. And to my astonishment, they refused me them and said I might go home without my children; and if I was not contented to live without them, I might come back and live with the Shakers.

The age of my children at this time was this—Caleb M. Dyer, thirteen in August; Betsey Dyer, eleven in January; Orville Dyer, nine in June; Jerub, seven in March; Joseph Dyer, four in February.[9] The Elders, "wondered why I came there with my unbelief, filled with my natural and carnal affections, and to think of carrying my children back; I was the most abominable wretch on earth; one who had the opportunity which I had, and be so unbelieving, it was terrible." One stamped, and told me never to presume it again; and "for me to think to carry my children away from the gospel, was dreadful."—Joseph was coming down to live as soon as possible. I must go home and take care of Daniel Taylor's family,[10] and my children should be no expence there. He called me a mean creature and said many other aggravating things. It appeared as though he meant to aggravate me if possible. I was sure I had need of much of that spirit that was able to endure all things. The scene was so horrible, that an adult sister who went with me to accompany me, wept like a child. I was obliged to depart, and leave all my dear children under the control of a people, whose tender mercies are cruelties. As I was going away, the Elders said, I must not expose their ill treatment towards my family; if I did, I should fare the worse. I suspected that Mr. Dyer was confederate with the Shakers, to thus dupe me, and confine my children in this manner, and thereby induce me to comply.

After I arrived in Stewartstown again, I strove to keep my grief concealed, supposing there was no relief for me and my poor defenseless children. At length, the agitation of my mind became insupportable. At a time, as I awoke from sleep, I was in a state of delirium for a short time. My husband said, he "had observed for many days past, that I was in trouble, and he was sure that I should be ruined in case it could not be removed." I wept, and observed that I dare not tell him my troubles, lest he should tell the Shakers, and it would make my case worse. (I was afraid the Shakers would carry my children at a distance if I made any complaint against them.) As he insisted on knowing the cause, I told him that I could not be separated from my children and live; and to go and live with the Shakers and endure their severity would be awful. I then related to him what the Shakers had said to me. Mr. Dyer said I should go and live at the Shakers and have the charge of my children until he could settle his business, and he would talk to them, and they should treat me better. He then moved me with my furniture to Enfield, in the last of January, 1813.

I was placed in a family of Shakers;[11] they said I must remain there until our property in Stewartstown was disposed of, or changed for some farm near them. They treated me kindly a few months, and I really thought them a good people. They frequently requested me to bear testimony of the way of grace; they said as I had been accustomed to converse upon the subject of religion, I could speak better to the understanding of unbelievers, then they could. Accordingly I did, and held to the doctrine of the New Testament. A person who once had belonged with the Shakers was so honourable, she came to see me; I conversed with her (she was at the time a member of the Baptist church.) She told me "she believed I was a christian; but I was not like the Shakers; and if I continued with them I should be obliged to renounce every thing I thought to be grace." I kept my mind concealed from every person. I argued against the Shakers sometimes, and at other times for them, that I might become acquainted with their belief. I had a good opportunity to inform myself; I improved it by reading their books, questioning and passing amongst them; during which time they requested me not to study the Scriptures, lest it would weaken my faith in them, and it was not necessary for my instruction, as what they said was the word of God.

I soon discovered so much familiarity and deception among them that it caused me to be anxious for my husband's return, that we might both be convinced of their evils, and make our escape. A house appeared to be preparing for our family.

My husband left Stewartstown in November, 1813, and came and took up his abode among the Shakers. But he was placed in one family and I in another, and my children and furniture distributed in the different families.[12] Meantime, I was not allowed to converse with him on the subject. I was severely disappointed in having my family separated. I knew not how to contain myself under the anguish of my heart, as I was a hundred miles distant from my friends and none to depend upon but those whom I found to be great deceivers. But as we were not allowed to shew our griefs to another, I retired and wept in silence, endeavouring as much as possible to be reconciled to my fate.

In a few days my husband came to live in the house where I lived. But the Shakers said "the gospel has separated us and we must not look upon each other as husband and wife; and if I wanted a favour, I must go to the other brethren; and if he wanted a favour, he must call on sister Lucy."[13] The following observations were spoken at different times, that "none were married but those who were united by orders from the head; and that the gift of God would find the man and woman who were created for each other"—and that "they would be placed together in their lot in the church, that this was the intent of God from the creation; the man was the head of the woman, and the woman was created for the man, and she was the *crown* of glory which the man was to receive in his redemption; but none was able to unite agreeably to the will of God, until the way was provided by their first mother" (Ann Lee) or "not as we should make choice, but as the orders were from the head."—They said that "a man could not be a real Shaker without a woman!"

At this time there appeared to be a man selected out who was filled with the spirit of *earth!!* and who was placed in every situation to see me and meet me, and not be discovered by the lower order. Through pretended ignorance I kept at a proper distance. The Elders said "Mary, you must not be so shy." I told them I was afraid I should do something wrong. They replied, "you must throw aside your fears, Mary, and obey us, and that will be pleasing to God, and you must not be so shy, but become acquainted or you will be sorry," and "the world's people[14] think we are afraid of each other, but they do not know the liberties which we take. Mary, you must not be afraid of loving the brethren, we think it a privilege for the brethren to love the sisters, and the sisters to love the brethren, and if you are faithful you will find the fruits of the gospel." As the Shakers pretend to deny this being their faith I can prove it by their publication.[15] (See pages from 435 to 440, with other places.)

The reflection of these things filled my mind with grief and despair, and I told them I was not fit for a Shaker. I was called upon at various times to confess my sins, and they were dissatisfied that I had no more to confess; and said "Mary, you have not committed sins enough to humble you before us; we had rather have thirty of the wickedest persons you can name, than one like you to make a Shaker of"—and "you must be separated from that spirit which you call God, and be filled with our spirit, then you will thirst for the same we do, and will be willing to comply." They laid my unwillingness to my conscience, and said, "It was Satan trying to keep me out of their kingdom."

I then questioned some of the lower order about these things, and they acquainted the Elders of it; and I was called to an account for it— They said, "Mary, you must not tell a word which we have taught you, for we do not teach all alike, but we instruct each one according to the situation in which we intend to place them!" These scenes were horrible unto me, and without doubt, they have been awoke many a night by my sobs and cries. When I considered the deplorable situation of my helpless children, who must be trained up to deny God, and be obedient to those Elders; Oh! thought I, if I could only escape with my children, my suffering would vanish from my mind.—I could not conceal my grief, and without doubt the Elders suspected that I was intending to leave them, and if possible, take some of my children. They then drew a bond which they intended should debar me or my husband from ever taking them again. For many candid reasons I refused to sign the bond, and stated to them the consequences, with all the persuasions that would be natural for a tender mother. They then artfully and subtlely said to me thus—"Mary, this is not done to take your children from you, for we be-lieve you the most fit person to take the care of them. It is only done for a trial of your faith, as Abraham was called to give up Isaac. If you will sign it you shall have the care of them." It bound as not to molest, though the Shakers should treat them ever so cruelly. They are not bound to educate the children, nor to give them any thing when they become of age, nor to keep them in case they should through misfortune become unprofitable to them—they might cast them upon the town, and they are under no penalty. The Shakers are very severe with children. My husband remonstrated against me; he signed it and compelled me to do the same. I had no relief only to weep.

They then suffered me to have more privilege with my children for a short time. They then took them all from me, and said, "natural affec-tions, must be destroyed," (see Tim. iii. 3.) and "you need not be anxious about the children, they are none of yours," &c. I was compelled to pass by them when they were sick, and see their wishful eyes follow me, and was not allowed to inquire after their healths. Twice they were so sick their lives were despaired of, and I did not know of it until afterwards, though one was in the house where I ate my food. Oh! deplorable to a mother! how can I write for tears! My grief overcome me to that degree, my health became much impaired.—The father and the mother of the church, or of the *meeting chamber*, came to see me.[16] They said, "we have got a gift for you, Mary, to take another step in the kingdom. Mary, the gospel has separated you from your family; you are a free woman; if you will have faith, you shall see the salvation of God. You never have been willing to give yourself up to the people of God, soul and body." I told them I was willing to do any thing that was right. They said, "You are not a judge of right or wrong, neither do you understand the Scriptures. You must be taught the way of God; you must believe, that when we speak, it is the word of God, and obey it as such. What liberty we give you, you may improve, and it is no sin. None can know the will of God but by us, there is no other way for salvation but this," that "we possess a fire that is Christ;" that "the word Christ means the anointing which the man Jesus possessed, and you are not willing to bear it, but you must seek after it, and labour to obtain it," which brought to my mind this passage, (see Romans chap. i. from the 20th verse to the end of the chapter.)[17] "This will induce you to enjoy heaven when you come into union and relation according to the order of God." I pretended igno-rance. But oh, I thought you were the basest of the depraved. One of the elders said, I must endure a certain scene to prepare me for their holy state; but he did not know as I should be able to endure it and live. Much more was said, but as I have already wrote beyond the delicacy of my sex, in order to give the reader a few ideas of their pernicious prac-tices, I shall state no farther.

After this, they became so bold I was obliged to defend myself. Let us be insulted ever so much, we are not allowed to utter a word of it only to our elders. I went to the elder woman; I told her I should not conform to their practices; that I would not live in such a manner, if any one pre-sumed to insult me again, I should make difficulty for them—(while I write, I can view them with disgust)—With this they were displeased, they used every art in their power to distress me. Many things are so un-accountably strange that if I should state them it would appear incredi-ble. My calamity became so great that when I saw ragged stragglers pass the street, I coveted their liberty and happiness. At times I would con-ceal myself to look to God for strength to assist me. When I returned, they would mock at me, and say, "Mary, how did you feel when you was kneeling down to your God; I do not want any other God to save me, only the God in my Elders." Through my trials my health still decayed; the elders said there was no cure for me. I frequently asked the privilege of taking a journey; to go to my friends, or to the salt water. They would not suffer it; neither would they let me send a letter, nor receive one un-less they examined it first. They forbid my opening any letter, if it was given in my hand, until they had seen it.

At this time I had an opportunity to send word to a near connexion, that I desired to see them. The elders found it out; they tried to punish me many ways in consequence of it. Among all my troubles, there was no grief so great as the thoughts of my innocent children being subject-ed to that people. They did not afford me any medical aid. I was obliged to leave them and go to my friends. Previous to my going, to avoid re-proach, I went to all the adults in the family to know if I had done or said any thing to offend them, the answer was, "nay, nay;" until I came to the Elders; they said "nay, Mary you have not offended, only you have not got our faith." The last time I had any conversation with my babe, one of the elder women came into the room with violence.[18] She raved and scolded at the child, and called him all the mean names; she caught hold of him and attempted to drag him out. The child was frightened and screamed. I plead with her not to treat him so. Her answer was, I will, he is none of your child, he is mine; she dragged him along. Oh! thought I, this is enough. This was Friday evening; I determined on going away as soon as possible. Saturday I took no part of work with the family. I was soon ordered to go to the Eldress' room; when I felt sufficiently established I went. I always was obedient to their common laws, as there was no other way to search them out.

They threatened me, they flattered me, but it was in vain; I told them freely I was going away. I desired to see my husband. I was permitted to in the presence of four Elders. As I wished to acquaint Mr. Dyer with my situation, I observed, that my health was so low I should continue but a short time if I staid there, neither could I be justified. Mr. Dyer said he was willing I should go away, and he could not desire any one to stay in the trouble I had been in for six months, from my appearance. I reminded him of his promises before I consented to go to the Shakers. He said he had as good a right to take the care of any other woman as of me; that I was not his wife, and as for the children, they were none of his to give; that he should lose his union if he did. Then I turned to the Shakers. I entreated of them to let me have my babe, and that I would get sufficient bonds that it should be no expense to the father of them; but no. I plead with them again, as I must be left destitute of any consolation or dependence in the world, I was willing to come on my knees and receive it as a favour, if they would let me have it. They heard to none of my moans or entreaties, but told me positively I should have none. O, what heart could endure it.—I felt the sorrows of an afflicted parent, bereft of her children; my case was desperate; to go any further from my children was distressing, to stay was death. Who can have sensations with me? Oh! can any? I think some mothers can, but they cannot relieve me. I call for the tender feelings of fathers to have pity on the feminine sex. Let me implore you to remove this heavy yoke of bondage, and break those chains which rend every tender feeling of the heart. I seek for a relief for my situation, and likewise a remedy against further evils of the kind. I cannot write for tears. The Elders charged me not to expose their practices, for it was a secret and the world never did know it, nor never was to, and if I told it they would deny it and make me the liar.

My husband was going immediately to the town where my relations were. I asked the Shakers to let me go with him, but they would not. The next day I made my escape with my youngest child, though there was a watch placed to guard me and the child. This was the only deceiving thing I did while I was with them. This was in January 1815. I had the comfort of riding eight miles with the dear little creature in my arms. The child said, "ma'am why did'nt you take the care of me when we were at the Shakers? The Elders said you was tired of me, and did not wish to take the care of me." How many lies has been told by these gracious people to keep my children.

In February my husband advertised me as his lawful wife.[19] In March 1815, I went with my friends and demanded his care and protection. He promised to take christian care of me. I was glad to go to my husband, have his care, be near my children, and not be compelled to be a Shaker. I did not fear the Shakers torments, if I was not obliged to obey them. They placed me in a room alone, and forbid my going into any other house or apartment; and said it was law for the wife to obey her husband, and if I did not do it he would not be obliged to provide for me. They forbid my writing or speaking to any person separate from the Shakers. They brought my food to me—they ordered me to spin tow.[20] My health was so debilitated that I was not able to sit up a day, without lying down a number of times to rest. I requested some sewing work—they would not permit it—and said, if I was not contented with my situation, I might go away and provide for myself. I told them I had rather endure any affliction, and have a home provided for me by my husband, than to be alone in the world, though I might be in better circumstances.

James Chapman usually attended my husband when he came to my room. This man was a stranger to me, yet he would talk abusively to me. Once he talked so abusive to me, my husband forbid him, and said it was of no service. I observed to Chapman it was possible he had a wife somewhere he had treated in the same manner. He denied that he ever had a wife. I afterwards learnt he had brought a number of children from his wife.[21]

After I had suffered much severe treatment in this place, which I will mention; while I was in this low state of health, my husband would come into the room where I was confined, and appear to be in a great rage; he would double his fist, and come towards me, and say, confess your sins, and join the people of God, or you will go to hell. At other times he would say, You must do more work, or you will suffer for it; I have a right to punish you as I would a child, if you do not obey me. I begged of him to let me live in peace, while I did live. It appeared my life was to be short, as I was placed. I was constant to work, when I was able to sit up. I would fall into tears, and ask my husband what I had ever done in my life that he should treat me so. He said it appeared to him sometimes as though he should die to treat me as he was obliged to.

I made it my home in this house ten weeks, and no person slept in the house but myself. My health was so low that I begged for some relief. They did not grant me any, and left me alone. My fire went out early in the evening; it was a very cold night. In the morning it was with the utmost difficulty that I dressed myself, and had no fire to kindle. I remained in the cold until eight o'clock! It appeared as though I must die there alone. They would not let me send any word, nor write a letter to a friend, nor suffer any one to speak to me from fear. They said, if I was not contented, I might go away. I told Mr. Dyer I was willing to suffer unto death, if thereby he would be convinced, and liberate the children.

It appears that Providence sent a person to see what my situation was. I was in hopes the Shakers did not discover him, and that I might be able to let him know my situation; but they saw him and come immediately. I had only time to tell him that I wanted some paper to keep a journal on; and further, if I had any friends in the world, I wanted two to come, and see my situation; and let me know what privileges the law allowed me. This was on Monday. Wednesday some persons came to see me[22]—they told me to take my liberty as I used to do, when in Mr. Dyer's care. I took liberty—walked out, and got sight of my children, but must not converse with them. I went twice to Hanover to meeting, though I was forbid going to any but the Shakers. I let the people know of the Shaker's conduct. The Shakers began to be alarmed—they said if I did not go away, they would take my children and carry them where I could not find them. Shortly after two men came and told the Shakers that they must treat me better, and that I ought to have the privilege of doing my own work, and to associate with my friends, and to know and see to the welfare of my children, and to go to meeting where I could answer my own conscience. The Shakers with my husband promised that it should be so. The next morning they sent my husband twenty-eight miles to hire my board.[23] They said this ground is holy, and none shall stay on it but the Shakers. I begged for one child, and observed, as I had staid and endured their treatment until they were obliged to treat me better, now I should not go willingly. They crowded me out of the house and obliged me to get into a carriage. My husband with James Chapman drove the carriage away. I continued in lamentation at the thought of leaving my children behind me; and begged that I might have some of them that I could know if they were alive or dead. My husband said, Mary, why do you weep so, you have done the best you could. He requested me to try every way in my power to obtain some of my children, if I could obtain one he would certainly leave the Shakers, then he should be convinced they were wrong. He was one of the best of husbands; and I verily believe he would still have treated me kindly if it had not been for the Shakers. My husband left me, and my troubles were such at this time, that I thought I must have lost my reason. I went back to the Shakers—they said my husband was absent—I wandered about the village to get a sight of him and my children, until my grief and fatigue brought on a sickness, with fainting, so that I thought I must fall down, and expire. I strove to get to a world's family for relief. I was a number of times obliged to lie down upon the ground, when I thought I should never rise more. As I was more acquainted with Judge Evans' family than any other, I went there.[24] The Judge is knowing to many of my sufferings in consequence of the Shakers' cruelty, and has frequently told me he thought I ought to have some relief, and has said he would assist me as far as was possible. Yet for some cause, best known to himself, it appears he stands militant against me. I am a real sufferer, and I need fathers and friends.

I returned to the place where Mr. Dyer hired my board, and staid until the time had expired, and got better in health. I again went to the Shakers, and told them in presence of Judge Evans, that provided they would let me see my husband and children, and converse with them, absent from the Shakers, I would leave them and never come near them more, they refused—I offered to converse with them in the presence of the Judge; they refused and he went away. They ordered me to leave their house. I requested of them to let me stay until the stage returned the next day; and that I had a right to stay where my husband was, but no. At length my husband entered the room in a passion, seized me in order to thrust me out of the door. I held fast to the door casing, until he tore my clothes very badly; one of the women unclenched my hands so sudenly that I fell backwards upon the floor. When I recovered my senses, my husband, James Chapman, and two Shaker women were standing by me; when they saw me open my eyes, they clenched hold of my feet with my clothes and dragged me out of the door, down four steps to the ground, then through the door yard, out of the gate into the street. They tore off my cap and handkerchief and left me sitting on the ground, and told the women not to let me come in. I spoke but twice—I asked Mr. Dyer if he thought it was Christ he was serving, and I told him I should not try to go in. I was past the power of anger or grief. This was in a cold evening in the month of October, and in this situation I was left without a friend or a home!!!

I saw my husband take my trunk with all my clothing and my mantle, and carried them out of my sight. In about half an hour my husband came to me and said, I "had better be going to some house for shelter." I asked him to finish my days, and as he had separated me from everything but life, I was willing to die in his hands! After this, my sufferings were severe; but the recollection of them are so wounding and distressing to me, I can write no further. When I reflect how I am cut off from the society of my dear babes by my once kind partner in life, I cannot express my grief! Oh! how heart rending, and no remedy.

The following is but a faint sketch of some of their abuses to children:—

The Shakers' abuse to children is severe; They were called up by a bell at half after four in the winter, and half after three in the summer. The second morning after Mr. Dyer left me at the Shakers, I was awoke by a bustle in the hall, adjoining the room where I slept. My impressions were that my sick son was in trouble. I went instantly to the hall; there I saw a small boy, whom I asked where Orville was—he said he did not know. I was providentially led to a large dark closet, in which I saw a person start. It was my son—I told him he need not fear, it was his mother. He smiled and came to me. I asked him why he was put there? He answered that he was cold, and there being no fire to warm me by, I cried, and Moses (a Shaker man) put me here and said he guessed that would warm me.[25] It was a cold morning in January, and he was not fully clothed. I asked him where the remainder of his clothes were; he obtained them, and I assisted him in putting them on, and told him to come out. The child dressed himself in a room without a fire—he then went thirty or forty feet from the outer door to wash at a pump, then returned to the hall to wipe. The latch of the door was so frosty I could scarcely get my wet hand from it—all this he had passed through when he complained of the cold.

The Shakers do not make allowance for children—they think they must be men and women. Persons who were eye witnesses informed me of a boy seven years old, and of a rude disposition, whom one of the Shakers took down by the side of the pond, and tied a rope round him and hung him on the limb of a tree, and told him he should stay there all night; when he thought proper, he went back and took the child down. After that they concluded they could not subject him to their minds, and they sent for his father, who was a shaker. The child was then put into a shop, there he was kept alone night and day, only when his victuals was carried to him; after that the child was sent to the world. This child had been so frightened about the world's folks, that he was unwilling to leave his prison and go.

I could relate many similar circumstances, but they are lengthy, and even the recollection of them almost overcomes me. If any one is punished it is kept from the knowledge of others if possible. The youth are stinted, until by faith they will do more than a common stint. They are taught to believe that all their extra work adds to their treasure in heaven. They have such faith that some work until a few hours before their decease. How pleasant and delightful is their outward appearance and all civility, while within are task-masters, bondage and slavery; and none are allowed to utter a word if many suffer unto death.—When the Elder was forbidding me to inform any one of my distress, he said if each were allowed to tell the other their trouble, their society would be broken to pieces in a month. Now though all are in trouble, none know of any but their own.

They are without natural affection. They have a kind of affection—they love the fair and amorous; but when they become infirm or aged they are set at nought. I think God loved good old Simeon when he was tottering into the temple and took Jesus.[26] I think Jesus displayed natural affection when he pointed his mother to his beloved disciple, and said, behold thy son; and likewise called her his mother.[27] It appears when he saw her grief he could not depart in peace and leave her without protection. He restored Lazarus to his widowed mother—he was an only son.[28]

MARY DYER.

AFFIDAVITS AND CERTIFICATES
᪉

Coos County, Jan. 25, 1816

This may certify, that I the subscriber have been acquainted with Mrs. Mary Dyer from her infancy, and that I have not known or heard of any immoral or irregular conduct or behaviour. Joseph Peverly, *Town Clerk, of Northumberland.*[29]

I, JEREMIAH EAMES, have been a near neighbour to Mary Dyer ever since she was born, until about fifteen or sixteen years ago, and ever since that time have frequently seen and heard from her; but in all that time never heard of her immorality or bad economy.

JEREMIAH EAMES, *Justice of the Peace,*
through the State of New Hampshire.

I SUSANNA, wife of the above named Jeremiah Eames, do testefy to the same. Susanna Eames.

I BETSY TILLOTSON, do testify, that I have been acquainted with Mary Dyer twenty-four years, and can witness to the foregoing declaration.

BETSY TILLOTSON.[30]

State of Vermont, County of Essex, Guildhall, May 22d, 1815.

This may certify to whom it may concern, that we the undersigned have been personally acquainted with Mrs. Mary Dyer, the number of years annexed to our names severally, and ever considered her to be a person of good character, and a person of strict truth and veracity; and one who has always been a faithful woman to her husband, and economical as well as industrious in her business while she had the care of her family.

MICAJAH INGHAM, *Judge of Probate, Essex County, 7 years.*
OLIVER INGHAM, *Judge of Essex County, 11 years.*
DANIEL GOSS, *Justice Peace, 6 years.*
MOSES MORRILL, *Justice Peace, 11 years.*
WARD BAILY, *Justice Peace, 30 years.*
CHRISTOPHER BAILY, *25 years.*[31]

I JEREMIAH EAMES, JUN. Justice of the Peace, do testefy and say, that I lived in Northumberland the most part of the time a near neighbour to Mary Dyer about 20 years, and likewise in Stewartstown about seven years, and agree that the above and foregoing respecting said Mary's character is true.   JEREMIAH EAMES Jr.

Also,

> ELISHA DYER, *Town Clerk, 20 years.*
> BRAZILLA BRAINARD, *10 years.*
>   *Selectmen of said Stewartstown.*
> JAMES LUCAS, Northumberland, ⎫
>   *Justice Peace, 30 years.* ⎭

We do testify to the above.

> NATHAN BALDWIN, ⎫ *Selectmen of*
> JOSHUA MARSHALL, ⎭   *Stratford.*

This may certify, That some time about the first day of January 1815, Mary Dyer came to my house in Hanover, with a child, and stated she had been living with the Shakers, and that their conduct and oppression was such, her health was so bad, that she could not stay with them and live; that they took her children from her. While she was talking on the subject of her distress, Joseph Dyer came in, and tore the child from her. She begged of him to let her have it; and stated, as he had promised before she went there, in case she was not contented, she should have two children, he three; and she wanted that one, as it was her babe. He refused her request, treated her violently, and went out. Her trouble appeared to be great, as she was from her friends, and said, he refused to take care of her. We thought her case hard, and that she was much abused.

> JEREMIAH TOWLE.
> DEBORAH TOWLE.
> *State of New Hampshire—Grafton ss.*

Then personally appeared Jeremiah Towle and Deborah Towle, and made solemn affirmation that the above declaration by them subscribed, contains the truth and nothing but the truth. Before me

> SILAS TENNEY, *Justice of the Peace.*
> Hanover, June 11, 1817.

Whereas, we the subscribers have this 6th day of March, 1815, carried Mary Dyer by her request to the people called Shakers, in Enfield;
and heard her make a lawful request of her husband, Joseph Dyer, for
that privilege, which he stated by his advertisement dated Feb. 1st,
1815, that she had left—namely, a place for her residence, and likewise
his care and protection as a husband: and this she desires with liberty of
conscience, free from the bondage of the Shaker's faith. After many objections, he consented, and said he would take kind care of her. She
wished to send a line back by us, where she had been living. He refused
her sending it, or any other word.

JEREMIAH TOWLE.
DEBORAH TOWLE.

State of New-Hampshire—Grafton ss. }
Hanover, June 11, 1817.

Then personally appeared the above named Jeremiah and Deborah
Towle, and made solemn affirmation that the above declaration by them
subscribed contains the truth and nothing but the truth.

Before me, SILAS TENNEY, *Justice of Peace.*

I, CALVIN EATON, of Hanover, in the county of Grafton, and State of
New Hampshire, depose and say, That some time in the month of January, 1815, I became acquainted with Mary Dyer, and understood by her
that she had lately come from the Shakers—that her situation appeared
very distressing, as she was out of health, and without a home or acquaintance, as she said her husband refused to provide for or protect her—
thatthe first of February following, Joseph Dyer advertised her as his lawful wife, and forbid all persons harboring or trusting her on his account.
She then returned to Enfield. From information of those who carried her
back, I thought it my duty to go and see her and know how her situation
was. I went—when I came there I conversed with her husband and some
of the Elders. I questioned them to know whether she had done any thing
to offend them—they said she was innocent of any crime, only that she
would not believe in their faith—and further stated, that any person could
not reside there unless they were of their faith, and that her torment would
be so great, she would be glad to go away herself. I was then permitted in
the room where she was, in company with a friend, as I requested to see
her. Two Shakers went in with us—they said no person should see her,

male or female, separate from the Shakers. She appeared to be glad to see us, and said, "she had been wishing to see some person, that she might know whether the law required her to be under the restrictions she was placed in," and added, she was forbid going to any other apartment or house, of writing or sending word to any friend, or speak to any person, unless in the presence of the Shakers, and a woman placed over her to order her work, and that no person slept in the house but herself.

CALVIN EATON.

State of New-Hampshire—Grafton ss. }
June 11th, 1817.

Personally appeared Calvin Eaton, and solemnly affirmed, that the foregoing deposition by him subscribed, contains the truth and nothing but the truth.

Before me, SILAS TENNEY, *Justice of Peace.*

I, MOODY RICH,[32] of Maidstone, in the county of Essex and State of Vermont, depose and say, That I was present and see Joseph Dyer and Mary Marshall united in marriage in the year 1799—that they lived happily together, until he joined the society of Shakers. After the difficulty which that circumstance occasioned, I went in company with his wife to Enfield, to endeavor to prevail upon him to treat her like a wife, and to permit her to see and converse with her children, but was unsuccessful. He utterly refused to live with her, and assigned no reason but his having joined that society. They would not suffer her to converse with her children even in their presence, although urged by her in the most pressing and affecting manner. I therefore brought her back to her friends; not, however, until I had offered to procure to them good bonds, to any amount, if they would permit her to take one of her children, conditioned that said child should be well supported, clothed and educated; which they absolutely refused. Since which time, I have frequently seen and conversed with said Dyer, and endeavoured to persuade him to grant his wife a support, but he persisted in declaring, "that he considers the marriage contract between them dissolved, in consequence of his union with the Shakers—that he did not consider himself bound to grant her any support whatever, and that he never would do it." She is now living upon the charity of her friends and relations. Said Dyer, previous to his joining the Shakers, was in easy circumstances, possessed of a handsome property which she had contributed her full share of labour, industry and economy to acquire.

Maidstone, June 7th, 1817. MOODY RICH.

Essex ss.—Guildhall, June 7th, 1817.

Personally appeared Moody Rich, and made solemn oath that the foregoing deposition by him subscribed contains the truth and nothing but the truth. Before me.

TIMOTHY FAIRCHILD, *Justice Peace.*

MRS. MARY DYER DR. to THOMAS J. TILLOTSON, & CO.
March 3d, 1817. To 4 yds. American Cotton

" Cloth, 3s6	$2.34
" 1 Bandanna Handkerchief	$1.13
	$3.47

I hereby certify, that in the month of February, A.D. 1818, I called on Joseph Dyer, the husband of the said Mary Dyer, for payment of the above account, and he refused to pay it, and further said that he should pay no debts of her contracting.

THOMAS S. TILLOTSON
March 9, 1818.

State of Vermont—Essex ss.
Guildhall, March 9, 1818.

Personally appeared Thomas S. Tillotson, and made oath to the truth of the above account and certificate.

Before me, TIMOTHY FAIRCHILD, *Jus. Peace.*

I, JOHN WILLIAMS, of Hanover, in the county of Grafton and the State of New-Hampshire, of lawful age, testify and say, that Mary Dyer, at the time she left the Shakers in Enfield, said she came directly to my house in said Hanover. I asked her if the Shakers lived or connected themselves with the women in the manner of the world—She told me they did not.

Question by Mary Dyer.[33] Did I not tell you at that time that they lived in a much more debauched state than to be married and have children?

Answer by the Deponent. Yes.

Question by the same. Did you not ask me at that time why they did not have children?

Answer by the Deponent. Yes.

Question by the same. Did I not tell you that they had to pass through a certain state of purification, which it would be impossible for them to have children afterwards?

Answer by the Deponent. Yes.

Question by the same. Did you ever hear Joseph Dyer say that Mary Dyer was never willing to give up her children to the Shakers?

Answer by the Deponent. I think I did.

Question by the same. Have you not heard Joseph Dyer say that Mary Dyer was a good wife to him prior to his joining the Shakers?

Answer by the Deponent. Yes.

And the Deponent further saith not.

The foregoing is according to the best of my recollection.

JOHN WILLIAMS.

State of New-Hampshire—Grafton ss.
Enfield, May 25th, 1818.

John Williams personally appeared and solemnly affirmed the foregoing affidavit by him subscribed is just and true.

Before me, JOSEPH MERRILL, *Justice Peace.*

[The above deposition was taken at the request of the Shakers.]

I, JOHN HEATH, of Enfield, in the county of Grafton and State of New Hampshire, testify and say, that when I was twelve years old, my father, together with his family, joined the people called Shakers. After I became twenty one years of age, I was called upon to sign the covenant, which they said I must do or be a reprobate; not knowing the effects of the law, I signed it. After this I lived with them seventeen years and some months; three years and six months in Canterbury, New Hampshire, for which I received some compensation; then fourteen years in Enfield, New Hampshire. From what I experienced while I was with them, I then told them it was my choice to go away and take care of myself, I could obtain no compensation for my work for the last space of time, although I was a hard labourer—the reason was because I had signed their covenant. This I think to be unjust, that they should bring children up in such ignorance, and thereby take the advantage of their hard earnings.[34]

JOHN HEATH.

Enfield, N.H. June 3d, 1818.

Grafton, ss.—Enfield, June 3d, 1818. Then John Heath, signer to the above, made solemn oath that the facts in the above certificate are just and true, before me.

JOSEPH MERRILL, *Jus.*

I, DANIEL PATTEE, of Canaan, in the county of Grafton, and state of New Hampshire, do testify and state, that when I was about nineteen years of age, I joined a Society of Shakers in Enfield; I continued with them about two years in Enfield, and then went to the state of New York to visit the Elect Lady, and the elders of the church. They assembled at their house of worship, in which they were assembled about fifty persons; there I saw Ann Lee locked in arm of a naked man; they placed themselves in the centre of the company. One man asked Ann Lee if he might strip off his clothes—answer, yes, you may all strip—and likewise all of the men stripped off their clothes, and continued in that situation, dancing and carousing for the space of three or four hours. I further state, that this, and other conduct caused me to leave them—as this was the conduct of the church and leaders of the Society.[35]

DANIEL PATTEE.

Canaan, May 27th, 1818.

State of New-Hampshire—Grafton, ss.

Canaan, May 27, 1818. Personally appeared before me the subscriber, Daniel Pattee, and made solemn oath that the facts in the above affidavit, by him subscribed, are just and true.

JESSE J. FOGG, *Just. Peace.*

A respectable lady informed me, that she was once a member of the Shaker Society, that they used much ardent spirit. One evening when they were gathered for a meeting, an Elder urged them to drink freely, until they behaved very indecent. The next morning, I heard one of the sisters say she was so drunk the night before, she knew nothing from the time the meeting was done in the evening, until next morning: then she found herself lying across the ELDERS' feet. The lady told me this, said that she did not like to have her name exposed, neither to have it degraded by the Shakers. She is respectable. I wrote this from her mouth as she spoke it.[36]

I, MOSES JONES, of Enfield, N.H. do testify and say, that I once was a member of the Shaker Society; and in the time I was an eye witness of many surprising scenes; some I will mention. When they were gathered in a meeting, they clenched a female of their society with severity, tore off her cap, pulled her hair, threw her down, kicked her, pushed her, dragged her round the room by her hair, and jambed and beat her to that degree, that it was with difficulty that she got her breath. They left her on the floor; and from her appearance, she was almost lifeless. I was surprised, and asked the Elder why they treated her so, he answered because she had testified in public as a duty, that their mother, or Ann Lee, was leacherous, and cohabited with the Elders. I see them attempt to cast out devils, to heal the sick, but to no effect. A woman that I was acquainted with from youth, which woman was a regular, steady person, until she, with her husband, joined the Shakers; after that, she become crazy, and continued so until her death. This woman was a subject of their pretensions in healing. This, with other conduct too indecent to pen, caused me to believe them deceivers, and I left them.

Grafton,ss.—state of New-Hampshire
    Personally appeared before me the subscriber, Moses Jones, and made solemn oath that the above deposition by him subscribed, is just and true.

JESSE J. FOGG, *Just. Peace.*
Enfield, May 30, 1818.

I the subscriber certify, that Moses Jones is a man of respectability, and is a Deacon in regular standing in the Church in Enfield, N.H.

JESSE J. FOGG

The Shakers Faith in man's creation and fall—taken from their own publication called Christ's second appearance.[37]

In man's creation, he was not completely happy alone, see p. 21, verse 5, 6. "But the Lord God seeing it was not good for the man to be alone, formed him in two parts, male and female, and these two parts constituted one entire and complete man. Page 7, v. 20, "Among all other living creatures that had yet been formed for Adam, there was not found an help meet, according to that order which was before him." (Meaning the eternal God calling him power and wisdom, or male and female.) V. 21, "And out of the man the Lord God made him an help meet, who was called woman." P. 442, v. 12, "Whatever essential glory man might have possessed, yet it could not have been declarative, so long as he existed alone; it required a suitable correspondent object to increase or augment his glory," &c. p.21 v. 6, "And in his capacity they were endowed with co-operating faculties, sensations and affections." P.33, v. 9, "Thus in the creation of man, his seed was in himself by the very law of his existence; and had his conduct been regulated according to the perfect law of nature, in the times and seasons which he appointed," &c. Now I speak of the fall.—I speak of the forbidden fruit, or of that part of creation which was to increase or augment man's glory. "I speak in a similitude, p.33, v. 5, would it not be just and right in a wise and prudent parent, who had planted an apple tree among the trees of his garden, more excellent than the rest, for the express use of his children, to lay them under an entire prohibition from eating or touching that tree until the fruit was ripe? And would it not be time enough for that prohibition to be taken off when the fruit was ready for use?" V. 6, "And should the children, through some disorderly influence upon their youthful appetites, be so deceived by the appearance of the blossoms, or green fruit, as to pluck and eat them, would not this be an express violation of the law of nature in that case, as well as of breaking the express command of the parent?" V. 7, "Here then would be the deceitfulness of the transgression, in corrupting their blood, and continually abusing the tree and themselves under the pretence that the father gave it to them, neither suffering their tree to bring forth ripe fruit, nor themselves to enjoy that benefit from it which their father intended. No union and relation could exist in order, until the woman was raised up in her appointed season, to

complete the order in the foundation of the new creation." V. 10, "Therefore, by the very existence of the laws of Creation, Adam and Eve were
forbidden to come to the knowledge of generation, until the time appointed by the Creator," &c. P.35, v. 20, "Did not Adam violate the laws,
and become guilty of the highest impiety?" v. 21, Nay more, was he not
condemned as a traitor? Yea verily, and actually banished from any right
to the tree of life. As it is written, Therefore the Lord God sent him
forth from the garden of Eden—so he drove out the man.

Redemption according to the Shakers Publication, or Christ's second
appearing—After Adam had lost all his right to the tree of life, (see
p.35, v. 21) and another was appointed in his stead, who kept all his father's commands, (meaning Christ) shewing that Christ was not a complete savior without the woman, (see p. 434, v. 4). The world is not one
person but many; yet all the world sprang from one man, who is therefore considered the foundation pillar or first father of the human race.
But as the first man was not alone in the foundation of the old creation;
so neither did Christ Jesus, in his single person, complete the order in
the foundation of the new creation, (see p. 455, v. 53,). The Holy Ghost
thus signifying that sin could never be taken away by all the blood that
could be shed, until Christ should come in the flesh of woman, (p.435,
v. 7,). And as the Church is not composed of the man without the
woman, that both are united in the Lord by an inseparable bond of
union, it follows of course that such a union and relation sprang from a
first man and woman, who were thus united, (v. 9) and as the order in
the foundation of the old creation could not be complete by the first
man without the first woman; so the order in the foundation of the new
creation could not be complete in the man alone; for the man is not
without the woman in the Lord, nor the woman without the man, (v.
8,). And whether they are immediately or personally known or not, yet
by the spirit of harmony and union flowing through the anointed, there
is a relative knowledge of their nature and union; as much as the world
relatively know of their foundation pillars, whose image they bare, (p.
552, v. 31,). But the truth is, as God created man male female, in his
own image and likeness, and called their name Adam—two in their order and manner of operation, but perfectly one in their nature and
union, constituting one entire man, perfect and complete in the order
of his manhood, so man in his first creation, in both parts of his man-

hood, relatively showed forth the glory, order and perfection which es-
sentially constituted the first cause, and was a pattern of that order and
perfection which was to be relieved by Christ in the new creation.

Now, my friends, as there has been much said by the world about the
life of the Shakers, you see they need a woman to be united with the
man, to be restored to that Paradise, that Adam and eve stood in before
they fell.

Now I will give you to understand how they are to be restored, and how
to abide in justification in the Shakers' way. As I have already shown that
Christ, in his first appearing, was not sufficient for full restoration, I further add, (p.455, v. 54) "And therefore the final expiation of sin was a full
and final confession of sins, and a full salvation from all sin is the consequence." Now by confessing your sins to God in their Elders, and walking
in obedience to the same, you must pass through a state of what they call
preparation or purification; then the man is restored to his proper lot in
their Church or kingdom; then the woman, which they call his crown of
glory, is given to him. Then they must continue in obedience to their
leader, which is God, and not gather their fruit without the command;
then they shall possess every blessing that was intended for the first pair;
in this is the complete restoration. In obedience, it is no sin.

If I had time I could shew you by their Book, that this is the full work
of redemption, and no one can obey God's commands but by them. Now
let them come out and own it, and not keep hid behind the veil. When
Christ was crucified, the veil of the temple was rent. You Shakers may
deny this, yet you know this to be true; this connection is not your worst.
But oh, horrible! the way you take to purify your subjects. I speak that you
know to be the truth. Think of the calamities and dissolution that pre-
vails among you on the account. Where it does not cause death, it de-
stroys the capacity of the youth. Myself, if I had not strove against you,
should have been under the clods before now. Oh the agonies I have seen
people in there on this account. Will not God cause a deliverance for my
children from these scenes. You Shakers, you know these things are so.
You sometimes call them the judgments of hell, or destroying satan in us,
&c. It is too much for a female to speak of your doings. I did not mean to
write so plain as I have; but when I know your conduct I cannot withhold;
you might know that you are sunk in the very abominations of hell.

I often thought when I was with you, and since I have come away, that if there was no other way for my children's delivery from among you, and to be placed in the liberty of the gospel only for me to give up my life, I would do it. May the God of justice govern the hearts of men, is my desire.

MARY DYER.

Concord, June 12, 1818.

As I am informed since I have come to Concord, that a few of the people have an impression that my motive in coming to this place is to obtain a divorce from my husband; it is a grief to me to have them so mistaken! I was very particular before the committee, last year, in my observations on this point.[38] My great object is to have the privilege of living with my children—if with my husband, it is well. But as he refuses by word and deed to take care of me, I want my children, and as much property as is thought proper, restored to me; and then give me power in law to govern it. Then I want a law passed, that no mother shall be obliged to part with her children in consequence of the Shakers, or of her husband's joining them. If the Court sees fit to take my fatherless and motherless children out of bondage, and let me be a mother again to them, I shall prize it more than all the wealth, or any other treasure on earth. I am sure my children are sufferers. Do have compassion on me and my children! I am thankful the Governor did not sign the act last year; as I understand it did not free my children.[39] If the Court would have pity, and grant me the power over the children, I desire that the Shaker's Society should be under a penalty (not the Elders in particular) until they bring forward my children and property; that the inhabitants shall not be troubled with searching for them, and to avoid their being carried away. This is my mind and desire.

One thing I will name, in Feb. 1817, Mr. Dyer requested me to get a divorce from him, that he might obtain an Elder's birth; and offered to find me expense money. But no; I respected my husband too much to give him up without I could obtain my children.

MARY DYER.

The following is the Petition of MARY DYER, for Legislative interference, on account of the mal-conduct of the Shakers, and their unjust detention of her children in their custody:

To the Honourable the Senate and the Honourable House of Representatives, in General Court convened—

THE Petition of Mary Dyer, of Northumberland, in the county of Coos, humbly sheweth—That she was lawfully married to Joseph Dyer, of Northumberland, aforesaid, in the year 1799—that they lived happily together in the matrimonial connexion for the space of twelve years, and were blessed with five promising children—that in the year 1811, her husband, the said Dyer, unfortunately attached himself to a Society of Shakers, established in Enfield, in the County of Grafton—that he afterwards, viz. in 1813, deluded your petitioner into a temporary belief of the rectitude of their principles, and the purity of their religious tenets, and she was induced, though with reluctance, to enter under the jurisdiction of the Society at Endfield; the elders having previously by address and deception, in concert with her husband, obtained possession of all the children.—That your unhappy petioner, having become completely disgusted with the Society on account of hypocrisy, the gross immorality and iniquity that she discovered in its concerns, and being anxious to open the eyes of her husband, that he might leave the Society with her, that the family might be brought up in usefulness to the world, was (as soon as her wishes were known) denied the sight of her husband, torn from her children, imprisoned in a solitary room, without fire enough, or the means of making enough (although it was in the dead of winter) to keep her comfortable, and various other abuses and indignities were heaped upon her, with denunciations and threatenings of greater torments, and cruelty, in the exercise of their vengeance, if she persisted in her intentions of leaving them. That she finally escaped from them, was pursued, and one of her children, whom she took with her, taken from her by force and violence; and the said Elders denied, and still deny her the privilege of taking from them any of her children, contrary to the express agreement they made with her, when she consented to abide with them—That the said Dyer refuses to perform any of the duties enjoined by the marriage contract, but he professes and declares that the same is absolutely dissolved—That although a compe-tency had been acquired by their joint toil, industry and economy, for the helplessness of infirmity and age, and which your petitioner had fondly hoped to have enjoyed, in the circle of her family and friends; yet after the said Dyer had withdrawn from her all means of support, and placed it in the possession of said society, he has prohibited publicly all persons from harbouring or trusting your petitioner on his account—This he did by order of the society, for the poor misguided man has no will, and performs no act but through their influence. Deserted by him who should have cherished her, and persecuted with malignant rancour by the society she had escaped from, your petitioner in sickness was obliged to appeal to the charity of her friends for aid and subsistence.

Such are the facts that have reduced her to her to her present deplor-able situation, and which she humbly hopes may be deemed worthy of legislative interference. And this state of wretchedness is continually aggravated by her reflections on the mode in which her children, if it should be their unhappy lot to continue under the government of this Society are to be brought up in darkness, in slavery, in the most stupid ignorance andfanaticism, in a manner that they can be of no use to themselves, or to the world; and more than all debarred the privilege of hearing without the walls of their covent, any explanations of the truths of the gospel of our blessed Redeemer, which might enable them to judge of the way they should walk, to obtain the best consolations in this life, and the hopes of happiness in that to come.

Your petitioner has submitted her unhappy case to the Honourable Legislature, confiding in their wisdom, justice and humanity for obtain-ing relief; and she humbly prays, that she may have an opportunity to furnish evidence to their Honors of these facts, and of far greater enor-mities that have been witnessed in the conduct and concerns of this Society, and rests with a humble hope that her cruel trials and sad suf-ferings may yet operate for the good of community, and be the occasion of some wise and humane legislative provision that will prevent the re-currence of similar grievances, oppressions and offenses.

All which is respectfully represented by their grateful and obedient servant.

MARY DYER.
Concord, June, 1818.

ᘙ

Enfield, May 28, 1818.

To the Honourable Senate and House of Representatives to be convened at Concord on the first Wednesday of June next.

We the undersigned beg leave to represent, That there is a society of
people in said town who are called Shakers, and by their conduct they
are disturbing the peace of the community at large. We have been visited time and again by women from a distance, crying in the streets, and
going from house to house mourning about their situation. It appears
that their husbands, their property and their children, are with said society of Shakers, and the women deprived of every earthly enjoyment,
and even deprived, without the greatest difficulty of seeking and conversing with those little babes, which we have reason to believe were
taken away by violence from their mothers' arms. We do believe those
women, (especially Mary Dyer, who petitioned to your honourable body
last year for some relief) have been abused in a most disgraceful and
shameful manner.—And, we do further believe that there is no other
Society within our knowledge that are so destitute of human feelings or
suffer those distressed females to be so imposed upon. Therefore we pray
that there may be a law passed touching their case, similar to a law that
has been passed in the State of New-York for similar cases, or take some
other measures to relieve them and all others in a similar situation, and
the community from hearing the cries of those distressed women. And
as in duty bound will ever pray.

Jonathan Jones,	James Huse,
Daniel Currier,	Nathan Currier,
Nathan Follansbee,	Richard Currier, 3d,
Davis Huse,	Joseph Merrill,
Silvanus Barnard,	James Willis,
John Heath,	Nathaniel Goodrich,
John Johnson,	Daniel Willis,
Daniel Stickney,	John Morgan,
David Noyes,	Samuel Hosmer,
Joshua Noyes,	Joseph Blake,

Joshua Martin,
G. W. Johnson,
Gideon Dickenson,
Isaac Jones,
Moses Jones, jr.,
Jonathan Sawyer, jr.,
Thomas Seaver,
Stephen Sanborn,
John Johnson, 2d,
Stephen Folsom,
John Huse,
Richard Currier,
Timothy Rowe,
Joshua Stevens

Benjamin Choate,
Peter Whittier,
Samuel Jackman, jr.,
John Jeffers,
Rowel Colby, jr.,
Matthew Pettengill,
Enoch Nichols,
James Morse,
Paul Chase,
Henry Currier,
Benjamin Blake,
William Huse,
Moses Johnson, 3d.

A

COMPENDIOUS NARRATIVE,

ELUCIDATING THE

CHARACTER, DISPOSITION AND CONDUCT

OF

MARY DYER,

FROM THE TIME OF HER MARRIAGE, IN 1799, TILL SHE LEFT
THE SOCIETY CALLED SHAKERS, IN 1815

With a few Remarks upon certain Charges which she
has since published against that Society.

TOGETHER WITH SUNDRY DEPOSITIONS.

———

By her husband JOSEPH DYER.

———

TO WHICH IS ANNEXED,

A REMONSTRANCE *against the Testimony and Application of the said* MARY, *for Legislative interference.*

———

CONCORD:

PRINTED BY ISAAC HILL,

FOR THE AUTHOR.

1818.

A

COMPENDIOUS NARRATIVE,

ELUCIDATING THE

CHARACTER, DISPOSITION AND CONDUCT

OF

MARY DYER,

FROM THE TIME OF HER MARRIAGE, IN 1799, TILL SHE LEFT
THE SOCIETY CALLED SHAKERS, IN 1815.

With a few Remarks upon certain Charges which she
has since published against that Society.

TOGETHER WITH SUNDRY DEPOSITIONS.

BY HER HUSBAND JOSEPH DYER.

TO WHICH IS ANNEXED,

*A REMONSTRANCE against the Testimony and Appli-
cation of the said* MARY, *for Legislative interference.*

CONCORD:

PRINTED BY ISAAC HILL,

FOR THE AUTHOR.

1818.

INTRODUCTION.

IT is with reluctance and deep regret that I now undertake to disclose to the public that *refractory and imperious disposition* which MARY, my wife, retains; and that extraordinary inclination which she has ever manifested to rule and govern those with whom she had any concern; which is already sufficiently manifest to the candid, who have become personally acquainted with her, and her scandalous reports and false allegations against an innocent and benevolent people, who to my certain knowledge have ever treated her and my family with the greatest degree of beneficence, kindness and charity. Till recently I have been resolved to make no public reply to whatever she might state or publish concerning me or the people with whom I stand connected; as I considered her statements too vague and contradictory to merit any attention. And the very reason why I now undertake so disagreeable a task is merely out of duty, from that respect which I owe to the candid part of mankind, who have been shamefully imposed upon, and whose tender feelings of sympathy, without doubt, have been greatly excited by reading those false and libellous reports published to the world in a pamphlet, falsely entitled, *A brief statement of the sufferings of Mary Dyer, occasioned by the Society called Shakers.*

It is not my wish to injure the character, or hurt the feelings, of Mary Dyer or any other person; nor yet to conceal my own faults: but as she and others have stated that we lived happily together previous to our coming among the Shakers, I shall firstly state in a few, out of many instances, our manner of life; and upon what principle we lived quietly together before ever we saw the people called Shakers; not by way of retaliation or revenge, but that we may take upon ourselves the errors which we have committed, and not palm them on the innocent.

It may be asked why this had not been published before the public had been so generally imposed upon? To which I answer.—As I ever considered a contest between a man and his wife the most disagreeable and shameful of all contests, I was in hopes that she would have been prevailed upon to abandon her pernicious practice of imposing her false coloring and lying accusations on the public without an exposition of her character; especially after the authority of the State had declared the matter not subject to legislative interference, and had twice given her leave to withdraw her petitions. Therefore it has ever been repugnant to my feelings to publish my family difficulties; nor should I have undertaken it now were it not to answer the loud call of justice to myself and the community in general; whereas the said Mary has made it her chief business for more than three years past, and still continues to fabricate and circulate censorious and false reports and even criminal accusations against me; and more especially against the society to which I belong.

A Compendious Narrative, &c.

IN the year 1799, I, Joseph Dyer, was lawfully married to Mary Marshall, whom I moved home to my house in Stratford, in the county of Coos and State of New-Hampshire; where for a short time we had no difficulty: but within the term of a few months one circumstance occurred, which discovered to me what I had to encounter with in her disposition, which was as follows: She requested of me a horse to go on visiting; but as I was importantly employing my horses, I told her that it would not be convenient to spare one on that day; with which answer she was highly provoked. I attempted to reason with her on the subject, but all to no purpose: she became more and more enraged, and said that I need not think to govern her—that she would not live so, &c. and immediately started for the river which was but a small distance from the house, with every appearance that she intended to drown herself. This being so sudden and unexpected to me, and considering what regret I must feel if she should make way with herself on this account, I immediately gave up, followed her and entreated her to return to the house, though she was very reluctant; but promising her that she should have the horse and do just as she pleased, she at length returned and became satisfied to think she had gained her point. I soon found that I must either live in a state of perpetual uproar, or else condescend to let her do just as she pleased and yield an implicit obedience to her in all things, and as I always abhorred quarrelling, I submitted to the latter and thought at that time, that of the two evils I had chosen the least, but I have since doubted it.

I further state that while we lived in Stratford we had three children, two of which were peevish and cross, and it was Mary's common practice, if they troubled her in the night, to hand them to me, saying, "Here! take your brats and take care of them—I do not want the trouble of them and you need not have had the trouble of them, if you had not been a mind to—it is all your doings," &c. Many have been the hours that I have walked the floor with a child in my arms, while Mary, refusing to nurse it, lay and slept as though she had no care for me or the child. In this situation, when worn out with trouble, care and fatigue, I have gone to the bed, awoke her and desired her to take the child and nurse it; when the only answer would be—"It is good enough for you—I do not pity you," and the like. I now leave the reader to judge what satisfaction could be taken in this situation.

Sometime in the winter of the year 1805, we left Stratford and moved to Stewartstown, where we lived until we moved to Enfield, where I now reside.

I shall now notice a few circumstances which occurred while living at Stewartstown, merely as a specimen of this woman's inherent genius. As I came into my house one morning, Mary was whipping one of the children severely—the child was screaming in a shocking manner; his eyes flew upon me for relief; but suspecting he had been doing wrong, and knowing it would not do to take his part, I stamped on the floor and told him to obey his mother. She continued whipping till her rods failed her and then sent for more; and thus proceeded, in this merciless manner, till this child, not then three years old, was so severely lacerated, that he carried the marks for more than two weeks.[1] Now I leave the reader to judge what this crime would have been had it been perpetrated by a Shaker, or admitting (as Mary has stated) that this same child, after arriving to the age of eight or nine years, was put into a closet for a few moments for correction, the crime in her view appears to have been unpardonable, although the lad has no remembrance of the transaction. I do not state this as an accusation against Mary, but merely to show to what degree prejudice will carry the mind, even to strain at a gnat and swallow a camel.

Another occurrence I will mention as a clear specimen of this woman's common deportment. The said Mary being of a covetous make, as well as of a malicious disposition, and not willing to do to others as she wished others to do to her, a poor woman of the neighborhood came one day to borrow our side-saddle, it being a second handed one which I had bought a short time before, but Mary refused to lend it. The woman then came to me and pleading her necessity, I thought it my duty to lend her the saddle, and accordingly did. But no sooner had Mary understood what I had done, than she came to me where I was at work and began to accuse me of having unlawful connections with the woman:

and stated that I had no business to have lent the saddle without her liberty—that I had let it go to pay for that which I was ashamed of, and many more hard and scandalous charges which modesty forbids me to mention: when the only crime I was guilty of was I had lent the saddle without her liberty. And further, she wished me to promise that I would not transact or do anything contrary to her will. And as her exasperation and rage on this occasion were so extreme, I once more submitted, and she at length became pacified and remained peaceable for a while. And this is the only way that she ever enjoyed any peace, that is, when she could have her own will and be sole governess over me and all other matters.

The next plan to which Mary had recourse, and which she attempted to effect by great ingenuity and artifice, is the following. Knowing that I was under great concern and labor of mind to find salvation from sin, she began her conversation one Sabbath as follows, viz: "As we feel it our duty to give ourselves up to do God's will, I feel as if it would destroy both my soul and body to live after the order of natural generation." My mind being very tender at that time, I frankly told her I did not wish to injure her nor any other person either soul or body. She strongly urged the propriety of lodging apart, to which I consented for peace's sake, and not through conviction, it being some trial to me at that time. This occurrence, which took place nearly three years previous to our becoming acquainted with the people called Shakers, continued ever after, except in a few instances occasioned by our being gone from home, &c. Being under conviction, and having no one to converse with after retiring to rest, my mind was taken up in the most serious meditation how I should gain full victory over my carnal and fallen propensities, and find salvation from sin. And as I had submitted to Mary in all things and she had managed all matters after the counsel of her own will; for a while she seemed to be very peaceable; and through her specious pretensions to celibacy and piety, I thought she enjoyed religion: and being convicted of my own defects, I esteemed her better than myself. This I manifested to several of our Baptist brethren, which only served to exalt and prompt her to a greater degree of ambition and pre-eminence: so that before long she could tell me when it was my duty to speak, and when to hold my peace. I soon discovered that she had a zeal which was not according to knowledge, although I kept it to myself. At length, Mary told me plainly to my face that she had no more affection or feeling for me than she had for any other man—and that she felt her union with Benjamin Putnam, a christian preacher with whom she had previously been very familiar—that she had for sometime felt her affection for me growing weaker, and her union with Putnam growing stronger: and her conduct was evidently congenial with these statements.[2] *See Deposition No. 11.* This was the very first of my discovering the cause of her declining to sleep with me.—Here I found her pretended sanctity together with all her religion to be counterfeit.

About this time the aforesaid Putnam was at my house for a number of days. During this time, in conversation he informed us that he intended to get married. This appeared to give Mary great uneasiness: and she labored hard to convince him that it would be very wrong for him to marry. And when he was about to leave us, she came and told me that she felt it her duty to speak some things to Benjamin which she did not wish me to hear. Accordingly she went with him to the wood, out of my sight—was gone some time, and then returned apparently under great trouble of mind, and told me that Benjamin was determined to get him a wife. Here I wish the reader to pause for a moment and consider what my feelings must have been at that time; to have my wife, my bosom-friend, who had borne me five children, desert my bed of choice, without any provocation, and plainly tell me to my face that her regards were withdrawn from me and were placed on another; artfully endeavoring at the same time to blind my eyes by a hypocritical pretence of their union being spiritual, or under the cloak of religion. Oh what heart-rending scenes I have passed through on this and similar accounts. To have intimated that I doubted her chastity would have been unpardonable. Consequently a quarrel must have ensued, which to me would have been like death, and which I was ever determined to avoid. Hence it is that I have borne it hitherto with silence, nor should I now lay these things before the public were it not that truth might do away error, whereas the unprovoked and audacious insults of this woman on a peaceable and blameless society, and her specious imposition on the public, have become intolerable.

Soon after this, we heard that the aforesaid Benjamin Putnam was married; and the next time he came to my house Mary's feelings towards him were very different. She had several disputes with him; and told me she had lost that union which she had formerly felt towards him. During the whole time of her intimacy with this man, it evidently appeared by her conduct that she only wished me out of the way. I leave the candid reader to judge how I must have felt under these circumstances.

The above plain declarations from the said Mary's own mouth to me of her feelings, together with her breach of union with the said Putnam after she knew that he was married, may plainly show what that union was!

This is that spiritual marriage which she has so assiduously labored to palm on the Shakers, which she had adopted some years before ever she knew these people; and of which she is the first and only author within my knowledge, as will appear more conspicuous hereafter.

At length a man came among us by the name of Lemuel Crooker, who professed to be a Baptist or christian preacher—a deceiver in very deed. Through this man's deception I have myself suffered severely. He was a man that fasted often—preached two or three times a week—made long prayers, and said much about religion, and also a great deal about the desires of the mind and of the flesh, &c. And by this suit of sheep's clothing, he crept in unawares and led captive silly women.[3] This man we received very kindly, and he made it his home at our house when he was in those parts. Mary and I were both very much taken in with him; often attending with him where he appointed meetings; which did not prove advantageous to us nor the people to whom he preached, as will soon appear. The said Crooker was at my house a great part of the time, as he said he felt greater union with us than he did with the rest of the brethren. I soon found that he extolled Mary to be a woman of great talents and piety, which took her feelings captive and they were very intimate together. At length they became so familiar together and so capriciously fond of each other, that some of our Baptist brethren were seriously tried on account of their conduct; and related the same to me. But not being willing that they should discover any jealousy in me, I plainly intimated to them that I did not scruple their integrity. Mary perceiving my attachment to Crooker so great, she became more bold; even to tell me *that God had sent a man to be an help meet with her in the gospel – and that the care of that people rested on them – and further that she believed my duty was to stay at home and take care of my family.* These things to me I confess were alarming—I did not say much, but thought the more. However she effected her design, had a horse and went abroad with him when and wherever she pleased.

At one time in particular she stated that she had a call of God to go and deliver a message to a certain people of the congregational order in Vermont. Accordingly she had a horse and sleigh, took a young woman with her and went to Guildhall court-house, a distance of 36 miles—delivered her message, and after having made great disturbance and tumult among the people, returned home. During this period of three days time, I was under the necessity of being detained from my business to take care of the children.

Another time, on one Sunday morning, Mary asked me where I expected to attend meeting. I told her in the back part of the town, where we lived. Well, said she, I feel it my duty to go with brother Crooker over to Canaan, a distance of seven or eight miles. For peace's sake, I let her have the horse; though not without some trial on my mind, which I endeavored to reconcile by a meditation on these words: *God will reward the righteous, and punish the wicked.*

These few instances may plainly shew that Mary's chief attention was to this man, while her own duty was neglected.

I further state, that a girl who lived with us by the name of Susannah Curtis, saw so much of their attachment to each other that it became to her (as she was under concern of mind) a grievance, to see Mary frequently retire to a private apartment in the house with said Crooker and there spend hours together, when they professed to be God's ministers; Mary the meanwhile neglecting her duty and also her husband, who, as she observed, labored hard and attended his duty. This girl's trial was so great that she informed me of it. One night in particular, as I came home from work, Mary and Lemuel were shut up together in a room, where they had been, as Susannah informed me, for two or three hours. I took the pails and milked the cows, it being time that milking ought to have been done had Mary been in her duty. *See Deposition No. 2.*

In this manner they spent a great part of their time; and their intimacy became more and more notorious and alarming, insomuch that our neighbors and Baptist brethren had abundance to say concerning their conduct. But as my mind was deeply exercised at that time with regard to salvation from sin, those transitory enjoyments, which exist only through time, did not have that effect on me which they would otherwise have had.

Sometime in the fore part of the summer, 1811, the aforesaid Lemuel

Crooker set out on a journey for the state of New-York, in order to move his wife to Stewartstown. During this journey he went to New-Lebanon, and saw the people called Shakers. And when he returned to my house I was absent.

In the course of one or two days I came home and found Lemuel at my house and Mary very much pleased with his arrival.

And after getting what information we could from him concerning the people, it was agreed on by all three of us to go to Enfield and see the Shakers. Accordingly in the month of July 1811, by a mutual agreement we made our journey to Enfield, where we were received with kindness and respect.

During this visit by our request, their religious faith and principles were laid open to us without veil or covering, which were agreeable to my own conviction and inward test of conscience. It is true Mary appeared to be under some labor of mind while at Enfield; but I am very sorry that her conviction did, neither at that time nor since, run deep enough to show her that the god of this world is not that God which the people called Shakers worship. For although she pretended to believe and embrace their faith at the same time with me, yet as her union which she called spiritual generally centered in one man and not in the whole body, the church; it is not strange that she did not find her favorite seat with the Shakers during this first interview with them; for her union was not yet broken off from her brother Crooker, which evidently appeared after we returned home.

They did not understand the Shaker's doctrine—They preached purity, holiness, and every attribute that was virtuous; and also to abstain from every thing that was sinful or unclean—and from that which would defile either soul or body—To take the life of Jesus for our example, &c.

They further told Mary that the gospel (according to the apostle) required women who were married to obey their husbands. And the last words to her were; obey your husband—be kind to him and your family—attend to your duty and God will bless you. Farewell.

This was spoken more emphatically, as Mary had previously told them she had received a call of God to preach; and desired the liberty and approbation of the elders to go out as formerly whenever she thought proper, independent of me or any other duty.

I felt very solemn, but I found the case very different with Mary; for soon after we left Enfield, she began to manifest a very light and carnal disposition. She appeared to me like a person who being of a loose turn of mind, after having been restricted awhile by civil company, was more loose than ever. This appeared to be the case with Mary. She accosted me thus: "Well Joseph you are a Shaker—you have no business with me now—I feel like a girl—I feel pretty much as I did when I was about fifteen years of age," and many more carnal expressions too unbecoming to mention, insomuch that her sister who accompanied us rebuked her for such basely indecent language.

I would ask the candid reader whether the conversation as above described, intimated that this woman was borne down with trouble, because her husband had joined the Shakers, as she has so plausibly and systematically pretended?

When we returned to Northumberland, where Mary's friends live, they very well knew that she spoke very highly in favor of the people whom we had been to see; not only in private but also in public; for we attended a meeting while there, in which she spake highly in praise of the Shakers.[4]

The above I think may be sufficient to show that she was satisfied at the time (as it is said) that her husband joined the Shakers.

From Northumberland we returned home to Stewartstown, where we found our little family well.

While we were at Enfield, the counsel of the Elders to Lemuel Crooker[5] was, to put his hands to work, and with his wages pay his honest debts—that in so doing he might feel justification, and not otherwise. This was very trying to him indeed, as he had ever been in an idle habit. However he made some trial for a short time; and as he did not find so much time to spend with Mary as formerly, their conversation was more at night, than in the day time.

I slept with Lemuel in one room and Mary in another. After we lay down, he and Mary would talk together frequently for the term of two or three hours. One night in particular, of which I remember to have heard Mary frequently speak since that time, as having experienced greater light and satisfaction than ever she did before.

While under an extraordinary operation, she would scream and groan apparently in great agony of mind, insomuch that I was almost affrighted. At length she came out of this ecstasy and exclaimed: "Now I am a Shaker." But what I have here mostly in view, is the nefarious conversation which took place between them immediately previous to this great change, which may be partially conceived by the following:

The said Crooker related how arch he had been in attracting the females in his youthful days, and carried the matter so far that decency will not admit of a description. And Mary took up the same subject and went to that length which language cannot express, without a breach of modesty. They then undertook to state that as their faculties had excelled all that ever was known in that which was natural and carnal, if those great faculties could be converted to a spiritual use, what high standing they might be in among God's people!

Soon after this conversation took place between them, Lemuel began to leave the field, and spend his time with Mary at the house as he formerly had done.

The reader can but faintly imagine what grief and affliction I have endured under these circumstances. When we were separate from others, Mary would argue against me, but when any of our neighbors were present, she would argue for the Shakers, and appear to be firmly initiated into their faith.

At length, I found that Crooker was resolved to take up preaching again in his former manner; at which time he entirely quit hard labor and occupied his time mostly with Mary as usual. During these scenes of trial, I found I had so much to encounter, both within and without, that I told Mary if she would live and lodge with me as other women did with their husbands, I would overlook all that was past and would go no more to the Shakers. But her reply was: "Joseph Dyer, you need not think to bring me to this, I will *die* before I will do it—Whether *you* go to the Shakers or not, I will never do it." This was but a few weeks after we returned from Enfield. The truth is, she always chose to be on the opposite side: this is her make and disposition. She always wanted to be disputing with somebody, and did not much care which side she was on, right or wrong, if she could only carry her point. This she has virtually acknowledged in her narrative, and says she did it to find out their errors. I should suppose that to be a ready way to find out error and not truth, for the truth is found only by walking into it.

In the month of August 1811, within about six weeks after we returned from Enfield, (according to the best of my remembrance) the aforesaid Lemuel Crooker, left Stewartstown. Ever after this time Mary professed to be fully established in faith with the people called Shakers, until she left them in January 1815: Accounting me at the same time as an apostate until I became reestablished in the faith in February 1812: the time she states that I called on the Shakers in Alfred, and returned home strong in the belief that they were the true Church.[6]

It is true, after attempting in vain to persuade her to live and lodge with me as a wife, I offered her two of the children, if she would go and live with the Shakers; but this she likewise refused, and so I found as always before, that the only way I could do, and live in any peace, was to let her have her own will and way in all things, which I did from that time till she left the people. There might be much said concerning my going to Alfred; how highly animated Mary was when I returned, confirmed in that faith in which she had been previously established; of a letter we wrote to the brethren at Enfield; how forward we were to have them take some of the children and how well pleased we both were when they consented to take an indenture of our children, with all of which we both acknowledged ourselves satisfied at the time; and if we were not, we lied and did not the truth.

But as the foregoing has been proved to a demonstration, not only by living witnesses but also by Mary's own hand writing, now extant; I shall add no more here respecting what passed before we came among the Shakers, but shall recur to a more recent date, as the foregoing is sufficient to show on what principle we lived quietly together for eleven years before that time.

After war was declared with Great Britain, in the year 1812, Mary and I both professing full faith with the people called Shakers, she was very anxious to move from the line, on account of the war, as she pretended. Accordingly in December the same year, as I performed a journey to Connecticut, by her desire I took two of the children to Enfield, N.H.[7] And it was an agreement between her and me to convey the children there, as the Overseers, out of charity, considering our embarrassments, had offered to board Mary and the children free from expense while I could turn our property and settle my debts, and thereby stop the interest, and in some instances the cost of suit; also that Mary might bring stock and work for herself. But all this was left freely to our own choice to accept or refuse.

Accordingly in the winter of 1813, I moved Mary and the other three children to Enfield, agreeable to her own desire, where they were kindly treated and well supported for six or seven months free from expense. I also had more than an hundred dollars of their property to assist us in our embarrassments, and many more favors too numerous to mention, which I trust in God I shall never forget and which merit our gratitude at least, if no other compensation. See dep. Nos. 1 and 6.

The unfeigned kindness, charity and acts of benevolence extended towards me and my family (including Mary with rest) by this people from first to last, have fixed those impressions of gratitude on my mind and memory, which I trust cannot be eradicated by all the hard speeches and false accusations that Mary Dyer can invent. See dep. Nos. 19 and 20.

After they had done all this for me and my family, and I had done the best I could with regard to settling my affairs, they proposed to me that it would be their choice that I should take my wife and family under my own care and instruction as I should think proper, stating that they should not charge or exact anything for the trouble and expense they had hitherto been at on their account. Accordingly I thought it my duty to bear my own burden, and went to Hanover, and other places in quest of this accommodation; but failing in my design I returned to Enfield. But Mary having been informed of this, tenaciously opposed it, and said she felt such union and attachment there, that she could not leave that family & go and live by ourselves—also that we were not able to take care of our family; and many more objections too numerous to mention. Here the reader may see that she did not feel that gratitude which became one of her profession; for had this been the case she would have been willing to have assisted me in taking our own burthen upon ourselves. My feelings were very different: I felt as though my brethren had already extended greater kindness and charity than I was able to requite, and that it was our duty to take care of our family in the best manner we could.

Finding that Mary was not yet convinced of her former conduct towards me and that she still retained an opposite feeling against me, I hardly knew what to do or how to express myself to my brethren. At length I told them, as she always had and still thought herself able to teach and lead me in all things both temporal & spiritual, and as her sense was so high, I was afraid to govern her and therefore knew not what to do. They considered my case and had compassion on me, or they never would have been willing to have taken Mary into their family. They told us that, if we freely felt to give ourselves up to become joint members of their family, and could feel the order of the family to be liberty and not bondage, and if it was our free choice to give an indenture of our children and thought they could bring them up better than we could—if this was a matter of our own free choice and request, they would consent to the same, and not otherwise. Mary, wishing to show herself first in all things, immediately accepted the proposal; with which I felt satisfied, and also accepted the same. We were both kindly treated in every respect, and here we both resided, till she, disappointed in not being a leader in the society, and failed in her base and pernicious attempts, (of which I shall speak more fully hereafter) absconded in January, 1815.

Although Mary well knew it was ever contrary to the faith, doctrine and practice of the Shakers for one man and woman to be joined together under any view of fleshly commerce, either lawful or unlawful, either carnal or spiritual, either actual or intellectual, yet she used great exertions to establish a system virtually tantamount to that of unlawful connection, or irregular commerce, under a cloak of spiritual marriage.[8] And had she effected her favorite plan to her mind, and duped the Shakers to a compliance, I have reason to think that she never would have left them.

This pernicious system appears to have been contemplated by Mary before she took up her abode with the people, which was first discovered as follows, viz. In the month of December, 1812, as I was going on a journey to Connecticut, she sent several letters by me directed to the elders at Enfield, dates of which were Nov. 1, 9, 10, 16, and 18th of the same year.[9] By these letters they suspected something in her very contrary to the faith and practice of the society, though written in a very obscure manner. Not being able to determine her meaning, they kept the letters till she came herself in February following, when one of the sisters, viz. Mary Mills, desired her to explain her meaning with regard to what she had written, but she being somewhat ashamed, at first declined;[10] but the said Mary telling her that it would give reason to suspect some evil in her if she did not comply with her request, she at length stated that she felt a particular union and attachment to a young man of the society, viz. John Lyon.[11] This is the man whom she declared under oath before the committee in June last, was selected out for her by the ministry. However, her acknowledgement made such a black spot in her character that her extraordinary abilities seemed to be put to the test to cover it over and make it appear something else. She said it was a spiritual union and maintained with her utmost skill that it was agreeable to scripture and the spirit of God. They told her they had no union or fellowship with such a faith, nor was there any such thing owned or allowed among the people, but every one that had the true love of God in possession, felt an impartial and universal love, which was not contracted to an individual, and if she did not abandon her false opinion, she could not abide among the people. This is what she has a reference to when she says, "The elders talked ridiculously to me." *See her pamphlet, p. 6.* But she has not stated what that ridiculous talk was, nor what those carnal affections were. If she had, the subject would have assumed a very different aspect; for she placed her affections on this young man, who, with the elder, had the care of the family. And as the said elder was supposed to be on a swift decline of life, of course she supposed the man whom she had chosen would become the head or elder of the family, consequently she would be the mistress. I call her *mistress*, because any woman who could obtain that standing, in such a manner, would be justly entitled to the appellation of mistress.

Although Mary was frequently told that her false system was nothing better than unlawful lust, and could not be tolerated among the people, but was rejected with abhorrence and disgust, yet she was unwilling to give it up, and labored hard to inject her nefarious stuff into the minds of young people and insinuate to them that it was agreeable to the faith of the society. *See Nos. 12, 13.* However, all her pretensions to sanctity and of being led by the spirit were of little or no weight to those who were acquainted with the effect which that spirit had on her conduct, which was plain to be seen even by her own and other children; for often when she saw her mate (for such she called him) go to the house on one side, she would post herself in the door on the other, exhibiting at the same time looks and gestures of wantonness, and like old Potiphar's wife,[12] cast her eyes on him from day to day—though he never had the misfortune to lose his coat, nor come in contact with her, as he always cautiously kept at a proper distance in order to elude her amorous designs. *See No. 1.* But Mary's whole sense being swallowed up in her favorite plan, she proceeded to erect it into a general system for the whole society, even to the mating of youth and children: which truly made her appear odious in the eyes of every chaste and true professor. But being detected by the older believers, and failing in her first choice, she made some further trials among the younger class, but without success. And finding that she could not propagate her favorite principle openly, she then undertook to insinuate it into individuals secretly; but these, not being willing to receive her doctrine, she told them that it was the faith of the society, only they were not willing that she should know it; although she had been abundantly told by the elders and others whom she consulted on the subject, that there was no such custom, faith or spirit owned or admitted among the people—that it was nothing more nor less than the effusion of unlawful lust or evil concupiscence. But Mary, being tenaciously determined to support her system, appealed for an interview with the ministry, (who have the first care and oversight of both societies, viz. at Canterbury[13] and Enfield) and having opened her plan to them, she received a reply similar to that above mentioned, in which they fully disapproved of her specious and false sentiments. *See Nos.* 10, 11. From this time, feeling in some measure discouraged as to drawing the people after her by her former efforts, she went on in a pretended union testifying both in public and private that this people were the only people of God—that this way was the only way of God—that she not only believed but knew it to be the truth—and that if she ever left it that would not alter its being the way of God, &c. In this she continued until about five or six months before she left the society.

At length, finding that she could not support her union with this people in hypocrisy, and finding herself under the influence and dominion of the abovementioned irregular desires which she had so long been striving to support, she said she thought it would be better for her to leave the society, as she did not feel contented, and that she could do it without any embarrassment had it not been for one thing, which is, (said she) "I have testified in public that I know this to be the only way and work of God, and people will come upon me to know why I have left it;" (observe what follows!) – "*but I do not know how to turn it.*" See Nos. 10, 11. This she stated in the presence of a number who are living witnesses; which plainly shows that she had not discovered any of those evils which she has since charged upon the society.—For if she had, it would have been an easy thing for her to have told people that she had found evil among them; but this it seems she had not as yet thought of.

Perhaps Mary may deny that she ever undertook to establish such a system; but it will be in vain, as there is sufficient evidence to support the truth of my assertions. *See Nos. 1, 10, 13.* She told me that there were no women among the Shakers but what she could compass, and that they were not able to teach her; but this young man was a man of talents and had it not been for him her mind never would have been kept among the Shakers. She also stated that to own her union openly to this man was the greatest cross that she ever undertook. And I conclude she never would have owned it had she not been blinded through concupiscent desires. But she used great exertions to convince us that this union was in the spirit—that this young man was her spiritual husband, and that the only reason why we were not willing to acknowledge it was because we were not willing that she should come into her place. But as Potiphar's wife cried aloud against Joseph—palmed her own guilt and base conduct on him and caused him to be imprisoned because he rejected her amorous allurements and made his escape from her; so Mary Dyer, upon a similar occasion, has cried aloud against the Shakers, and has endeavored to throw back her own vile character upon them, because John Lyon, with like vigilance and promptitude has rejected her amorous allurements with abhorrence and disgust.

This is solemn truth. And here lies the very seat of her complaint: but God will reward the righteous and punish the wicked. He will protect the innocent and upright in heart against the malice of a sinful woman who has indeed, with open eyes, undertaken to change the truth into a lie; and that for no other reason that merely to satiate her own malice. And as the said Mary has advised the Shakers in the public papers to quote the first chapter of Romans[14] instead of the seventh of Corinthians,[15] here seems to be a suitable place; for not to mention her unseemly conversation and her continual attempts to inculcate licentious principles in the minds of young people, her conduct was so extremely vile and contrary to nature that a young woman by the name of Sarah Curtis, who was her bed mate, could not endure it: and requested to be released from the burden of lodging with her. The aforesaid Sarah Curtis, in conversation with Mary concerning her immoral behavior, told her it was such that she could form no very favorable opinion of her.

Mary's replies in vindication of her own foul conduct, as she could not deny it, are too shameful and disgusting to repeat, and much more so to publish; but let it suffice to say that as she had rejected all moral virtue and conviction, she was given over to a reprobate mind to do those things which were not convenient. See Romans 1, 26.[16] Perhaps some may think that I have carried these things too far; but as Mary has called upon us to let her know what her unseemly conduct is, I felt it my duty to tell the truth as far as modesty will admit. *See Sarah Curtis' deposition, No. 1.*[17]

During this woman's residence with this society her jealousy, (as might reasonably be supposed) was so extreme that she would frequently be roving from place to place and listening at the doors of other apartments watching for some occasion whereby she might propagate mischief and excite false jealousy among others: though she had but very little influence among those who understood her disorder. Thus she proceeded in this shameful manner till she became entirely blind to that modesty which becomes one of her sex. And notwithstanding all this, she at the same time and under the same influence of jealousy had great pretensions to the light of revelation. I will relate one instance of this nature which may serve as a true specimen of many more. One morning she came to me, apparently in great distress, and said her youngest child was dying—that God had revealed it to her—and that she had felt his situation all night. I attempted to pacify her, but to no effect. I then told her that her god was a lying god, and asked her if she would believe and follow him any longer, if I would prove him to be such? for I was well acquainted with her false revelations. I then immediately went to the bed, dressed & brought the child to her perfectly well; and told her she might see that her god had told her one lie at least: and as his revelations were false, I desired her to follow him no longer, but to compose herself and be a happy woman. This I suppose is what she alludes to where she has stated in her pamphlet, that they said she must leave her God and worship the Shakers' God; which bears as true a color as any thing else that she has stated concerning the Shakers.

To state all the particular conduct and artifice of this woman, with regard to her contemplated superiority over the society, would require a large volume; but the few sketches above stated, may show the candid reader, that her whole difficulty originated in false jealousy and disappointment. Had the Shakers resigned to her all they had acquired for more than thirty years—permitted her to have introduced and established her spurious system of spiritual marriage—acknowledged and proclaimed her lordess over God's heritage—doubtless she would have thought they had done her justice. Her own brother told me, previous to our coming to Enfield, that if the Shakers did not do this she would not stay long among them.

Mary, finding all her attempts in vain to dupe this people under her control and having lost her confidence by means of her base conduct, manifested a desire to leave the society, which she stated in the presence of me and a number of others. This was in January 1815. No one made any objection to her going; but we desired her to go in quietness. She said she would, and further stated that she could not say any thing against the people, for she had never seen any evil among them: but they had always treated her kindly and she meant to treat them so. I told her that she ought to have liberty of conscience as well as I: also that I was willing to come to an honorable settlement and chose that she should have her full and just portion of property and that we might each enjoy our own faith. She replied that she did not care about property, she could take care of herself. She then proposed to me to let her have part of the children. I told her I could not, for we had mutually given them up to the care of the society, and had obligated ourselves not to take them away so long as they were contented. She then concluded to write to Hanover in order to know what accommodations she could have among her friends.

Next day, being Sabbath, all the family went to meeting except one aged man and two or three children, one of which was our youngest. When the people began to return from meeting, Mary stopped a sleigh going to Hanover under pretence of sending on her letter. She ran in and told the aged man before mentioned, that she wanted to send a letter by those in the road and wished him to draw some cider for them while she got the letter: but as soon as he was gone out of sight—she caught the child, carried him out to the sleigh—got aboard and went off in that manner. I soon had information, and considering myself responsible for her conduct, I pursued her and brought back the child which I felt to be my duty. This is what she calls being torn from her children.

Finding that she was determined to trouble me as much as lay in her power, I considered it my lawful right and duty to advertise her to prevent further difficulty.[18] But when she found that she could not have so large a scope to trouble me as she expected, she came and tendered herself upon my advertisement, promising obedience as my lawful wife before evidence; which she has never performed. However, I complied with her request and agreed to take care and provide for her as my lawful wife, according to what the law enjoined on me in the marriage contract, provided she would yield obedience. Accordingly, I provided a comfortable and convenient room for her with free access to the highway, dooryard and kitchen, where she had her victuals provided, with full liberty to go as often as she needed any thing to eat or drink. I required no hard work of her except to wash her own clothes when she was well; and no more labor of any kind than what she was able to perform, which was left to her own discretion. And the only work she did, of my providing, was to spin twenty run for the term of ten weeks, the rest of her time being taken up in fabricating and circulating her scandalous falsehoods against me and the society.

I also provided a young woman to wait on her in case she should be unwell in my absence, from which she has taken occasion to say, there was a mistress set over her.

I further state, that during her residence in this situation for about ten weeks, which she has been pleased to call imprisonment, I provided her with a horse once, if no more, to go to Hanover, exclusive of her going once or twice in the stage: and not only so, but she visited different parts of the town of Enfield and other places just when she pleased: yet she has stated that she was forbid to write or speak to any body but the Shakers. Nor was there ever a lock or bolt turned against her or fastenings of any kind during the whole time of her pretended imprisonment, unless she had the full means to govern the same: notwithstanding her delusive pretensions to the contrary.

Soon after Mary tendered herself upon my advertisement, finding by her writings and conduct that she was determined to make me all the trouble she could, and that she had formed a connexion with a number of designing men at Hanover and other places for the purpose. I advertised her again to prevent further trouble, forbidding all persons harboring or trusting her on my account, as I had made ample provision for her. She was frequently visited by those of the above description who I perceived were plotting mischief against me. At one time in particular, on going to the room which she occupied, I found that she was fastened up with a young man from Hanover. I demanded my right of admission, which after some time was granted. On going in I found the aforesaid young man sitting before the fire and immediately asked him what his business was there with my wife, fastened up in such a manner: I also requested him to tell his name. To which he replied, "I do not know as I am obliged to let you know my business or to tell you my name." But I told him that he was in my custody, and I should keep him till he did. He was very impudent and said the company who sent him told him to stand them old fellows up well: and it seemed that he thought the more saucy he was the more faithfully he was performing his duty. But he soon found that I was not at play with him and concluded to tell me his name and let me know his pretended business. See dep. No. 7.

I told him that as Mary had formed a connexion with a number of men at Hanover, who were prejudiced against me, among whom he was one, I did not allow them to come one after another and be fastened up with her in that manner, as I was suspicious of their evil designs; but if Mary chose to go and take care of herself, she might have her just portion of property and form a connection with whom she pleased. After a short discussion on the subject this man finding himself in dirty business and that there was evidence of it, went off much chagrined at his ill success. During this transaction Mary was throwing out the most scandalous invectives against the Shakers and against me, which seemed to be excited only because I had found her in such a nefarious business. In this manner she went on during the whole time of her pretended imprisonment, seeking every occasion to accuse and stigmatize me and the people. One time in particular, just as the ground was opening in the spring, when no discreet person would consider it safe for a woman to ride, she requested of me a horse to go to meeting, a distance of eight or nine miles. I replied, it is not prudent, the going is so extremely bad: and not only so you say you are unwell. In a few days time she reported throughout the vicinity that she asked for a horse to go to meeting, and the Shakers would not let her go. And doubtless from this circumstance she has had the audacity to state in her pamphlet that she was forbid to go to any meeting but the Shaker's.

She has stated that she was constant at work when she was able to set up: This is true, but it was in fabricating and writing the most false and scandalous defamation against the Shakers without any just cause; and gadding from place to place to circulate the same. Thus she continued in her malicious proceedings, propagating falsehoods and exciting disturbance and tumults both in the family and vicinity until her conduct became intolerable. And as I had taken the room for no longer time than during her good behavior, the overseers of the family desired me to provide a home for her somewhere else, and take her from their premises, for her conduct was such they could no longer endure it. Accordingly I went and provided a home for her at Obadiah Tillotson's in Orford, a man in good circumstances, and whose wife is her own sister. I agreed to pay him for her board at the rate of a dollar per week for all the time she was there. But when I returned and told Mary that I had made provisions for her at her sister's, and that I would let her have household furniture, principally a bed and bedding, the best of the furniture which we had, amounting to more than fifty dollars at her own appraisal and five dollars in cash for expenditure—strange as it may seem, notwithstanding all her pretended imprisonment and ill treatment among the Shakers, she utterly refused my provision, and said she would not comply with any of my proposals. At length after much noise and tumult, finding her pretences to abuse and imprisonment cut off, and that my provision for her among the Society was at an end, she concluded to go with me to the aforesaid Tillotson's. Accordingly I provided a suitable carriage, took her with her furniture and conveyed her to the place which I had appointed.

Having become acquainted with Mary's attachment to other men, and also perceiving according to her own testimony & conduct that her affections were wholly withdrawn from me and that she was seeking occasion against me, and was determined to trouble me all she ever could; Therefore I was determined not to transact any business or be with her alone, ever after her first absconding: and more especially after finding she had attracted the attention of a number of men to wait on her, with whose names and characters I was not acquainted. For being suspicious of her evil designs, I was determined to give her no occasion to accuse me falsely; as I found that, to support one was trouble enough, in this disagreeable situation. Hence it was that I declined to do any business with her without witness. From this it appears she has undertaken to state that the Shakers would not let, or allow me to speak with her alone; or to do this, that and the other, which is entirely false, for they never did control, dictate, or even counsel me in any matter respecting my business with her after she renounced her pretended faith with them: nor did they *ever* advise me to anything inconsistent with my lawful duty towards her or any other person. But Mary being greatly irritated because I was aware of her ill designs, and took caution to prevent greater troubles, was determined if possible to overcome me in this point. Accordingly on the 2d, or 3d day of October, 1815, she came to Enfield in the stage, and entered the house of the family where I lived (even without so much liberty as that obtained by knocking) took a seat and went to knitting (having her work with her.) After remaining some time in this situation and not making known any business, one of the sisters asked her what she wanted? She replied it was nothing to her. The woman then told her as she was placed in care in that family she thought she had a right to ask the question as she came there in such a manner. But Mary appeared to be displeased and gave her no direct answer.

At length Edmund Lougee who was the head of the family asked her if she wished to see any particular person there.[19] She then replied that she wanted to see me. Immediately I was called for, and on asking her what she wanted of me, she answered: " I have no business to do with you among the Shakers—my business is with you alone." But I told her as I had often done before, that I should do no business with her in private. She replied, that she would not leave the house till I would. I told her if she would go to the Office (a place to transact public business about sixty rods distant) I would attend to her there and do any business that was consistent.[20] But this she obstinately refused. Those who had the care of the family used their utmost entreaties and persuasions to introduce her to comply with my request, observing at the same time that if I was scrupulous with regard to the impropriety of doing business or being with her alone they had no right or disposition to control me. But notwithstanding all their entreaties and reasonable persuasions, she continued obstinate, and in language very abusive from 10 oclock, a.m. to 3, p.m. At length seeing the disorder and confusion the family were thrown into by her clamor, threats and disorderly behavior, and finding all attempts in vain to compose her, Edmund Lougee, who had the care of the family, said that it could no longer be borne, and that it was their

right and duty to govern their own house and keep good order: and desired me if possible to take Mary from the house peaceably. After using
my utmost persuasions and entreaties to induce her to condescend to go
with me, and finding her obstinate, declaring that she would not leave
the house, I took her up carefully & carried her out of the house and set
her down without the gate, and desired her to walk up to the Office; but
she said she would not. I then prepared a horse and waggon and desired
her to get in and ride to the aforesaid Office: but she pointedly refused
and said she would not. I then desired James Chapman to assist me and
help me put her into the waggon which he did in a careful manner. I got
into the waggon, took her into my lap, held her carefully and James
drove the waggon to the Office, where she got out, and went in peaceably,—became very calm and was comfortably taken care of during the
night. We spent the evening in peace and cordiality. The next morning,
by her free consent, I provided a carriage and conveyed her again to Orford, & paid the aforesaid Tillotson for what he had boarded her; and
made further provision for her. I also gave her six dollars in cash and
told her if she wished to visit her mother and friends at Coos, I had no
objection.[21]

A great part of the said Mary's statement relating to the above transaction is entirely false, and the whole colored in a high degree, for although she has stated that one of the women unclenched her hands and
she fell backward on the floor, I can prove that no part of her body
touched the floor nor was she dragged out of the house or abused in the
least, but I carried her out in the most tender manner possible under the
above disagreeable circumstances, although she strove against me as far
as she was able. One circumstance which will go far in shewing how
great were the sufferings and terrors of Mary at that time, is as follows:
When riding from the house to the office, at the time I held her in my
lap, she looked me in the face, and jocosely observed, "I guess you are
afraid of a woman."

The above is a true statement of facts respecting this extraordinary
circumstance, which I can substantiate by legal authenticity. See dep.
No. 13.

Some time in the following winter, viz. 1816, I went to Orford, and
found that Mary had left her home and gone to Coos. As she had declined to live with the aforesaid Tillotson, I then agreed with a Captain

Page of Lancaster, Coos County, to board her one year, at one dollar per week, and obtained of him the conditions of the agreement in writing. The said Page had a convenient house and good accommodations as he had no family excepting himself and wife; he also lived on the main river road, about a mile from the court-house. Mary went immediately to the said Page and disannulled the agreement, declaring that she would not consent to the provision which I had made. Accordingly Judge Rich of Maidstone, Vt. who is her brother-in-law, came with her to Enfield, and demanded of me her support.[22]

I then agreed with the said Rich, and gave him my obligations for fifty-two dollars to provide for her one year, which I paid according to agreement. And notwithstanding I treated him and Mary with kindness and respect, and attended with them in seeing and conversing with my children to their full satisfaction, as they both acknowledged, yet he has stated in his affidavit that they would not suffer her to converse with her children even in their presence although urged by her in the most pressing and affecting manner—and that he was unsuccessful, &c. *See dep. Nos. 17, 18, 19, 20.* And whereas the said Rich, and others have stated that I have refused to grant Mary a support; I can prove that I have paid out for her support $124.80 cts. exclusive of being put to the cost of more than an hundred dollars in time and expense on her account, when at the same time it was evident that she was well able to and did support herself, and laid up her money; while I at the same time was under the necessity to borrow money to discharge certain debts which she and I mutually contracted before ever we came among the people.

After the time was expired for which I agreed with the said Rich, to board Mary, finding that he and others were co-operating with her, in order to injure me as far as they were able, I told them I did not feel it my duty to provide for her among those whom I considered to be my enemies; as the aforesaid Rich had boasted of the money that he and Mary's friends had, and said that he would injure me as far as he had power. And although Mary has always refused to come to any just settlement, which I have frequently offered to leave out to the judgment of impartial men, yet I have never declined to grant her a support according to the best of my circumstances, provided that she would live where I could do it with safety. But I told her I did not consider myself obligated, neither should I support her any longer in connexion with those who were ill disposed and who had threatened to do me all the injury they could. But she was highly displeased and utterly refused to comply with any of my lawful demands, or reasonable proposals; and through the aid and instrumentality of those who were my enemies, and with whom she was combined, has petitioned the authority for legislative interference under pretence of intolerable grievances. She has laid two petitions before the legislature of this State, and had leave to withdraw the same. She has maliciously put the State to the cost of perhaps two thousand dollars for no other cause than that of getting her will, and seeking revenge against me and the society to which I belong, and that without any provocation. Ever since the spring of the year 1817 this woman has been posting from place to place spending her time in writing and publishing the most scandalous and groundless falsities against me and the Shakers; during a part of which time she made it her rendezvous at the house of James Willis, in Enfield, who, it appears has aided and assisted her in getting her pamphlet printed, &c.[23] And notwithstanding I had twice legally advertised her and forbid all persons harboring or trusting her on my account, yet the said Willis has unwarrantably trusted her on my credit, and let her have tape, lace, cambrick, calico and such like articles to the amount of about twenty collars, without my liberty, and has sued me for the same, as if he would wish to wrong me out of what little property I have.[24] I do not wish Mary Dyer to wrong any man on my credit, neither do I feel it my duty to follow her from place to place to protect and support her, seeing she has refused to comply with any of my reasonable and lawful demands. But if she will behave herself in a becoming manner, let me know where the bed and other furniture is, which she has secreted, and put her hands to work no harder than I do, according to her strength, I will take care of her and treat her kindly, which I never refused to do on these conditions. And if she is not disposed to comply with this offer, and the above conditions do not suit, I will come to an honorable settlement, and let her have her full proportion of property, provided I can be sufficiently indemnified.

The said Mary has manifested great anxiety and concern about the children; pretending that if she could obtain them or a part of them she would be satisfied; but if I may be allowed to judge from her former words and conduct with regard to the children, I must conclude that her great concern is spurious; for she has not performed the duty of a mother towards her children. But admitting her pretensions to be real, I would ask any man who has the best regard for christianity or moral virtue, if he could justifiably relinquish his unalienable right of care or the protection and welfare of his children, and delegate it to a woman whose immorality, impiety and base conduct has far exceeded any thing that I have hitherto stated.

Therefore as I have the first and exclusive right, with regard to the protection and well being of my children, vested in me not only by the laws of man, but by the Creator, and considering that I must be accountable to him for all my doings, I cannot sacrifice this right or transfer it to Mary Dyer, even if it were in my power, without a pointed violation of my own conscience.

But as we have mutually and freely given our children up to the care and protection of the society by indenture, agreeably to my faith and their own free choice, and have obligated ourselves not to molest or take them away while they were contented,[25] I have neither the power nor will to break my solemn covenant or to use any influence whatever, to cause them to abandon that which I conscientiously believe to be for their greatest and only eternal good. And the aforesaid agreement, which is equally binding on the part of the society and which obligates them among other conditions to give me notice or deliver the children up to me in case they should be discontented: this I hope and trust they will keep accordingly. And should any of the children break the conditions of agreement or be discontented so as to come under my care and protection, my conscience would forbid that I should transmit the care of them to Mary Dyer, (or to any other person of a similar character) except she greatly reform her life and conduct, as I could not be justified in so doing: for I consider that I must be accountable to God, as well in regard to the instruction and welfare of my children, as for any thing else. But did she in this case hold the prerogative and first right of care, I should be clear, let the consequences be what they might.

My children are all contented and greatly satisfied with the home and provision I have made for them, being kindly treated, well educated and instructed in everything that is virtuous; and their only grief is, to see the unprovoked malice and abusive conduct of their mother against me and the society under whose care and protection they are placed. And although it was not stipulated in the indenture given of the children for my daughter to be instructed in the knowledge of arithmetic; and probably thereby some have taken occasion to publish that the Shakers did not instruct their females in that science, yet, previous to such reports, my daughter had been instructed by the society to a competent knowledge of the four ground rules of arithmetic, both with regard to whole numbers and also decimal fractions; and the females were generally instructed in that art, according to their capacity, equal with the males.[26]

It may be observed that the said Mary, in the greatest part of her assertions relating to circumstances transacted both before and after she left the said society, has made use of the plural pronoun, "they," meaning the Shakers: as, "they would not let me go"—"they forbid my writing or speaking to any but the Shakers"—"they placed me in a room" "they would not permit it," &c. as if the Shakers did or said so and so—which is a plan of deception calculated to give her statements a color in the eyes of the public. This plan she fully adopted at the time she tendered herself in order to seek some occasion against the society: but the truth is, they never did dictate or meddle with her after her first absconding, unless she intruded herself into their buildings and affairs; nor have they ever directed or dictated me in relation to my proceedings with her, any further than to counsel me to do my duty to her in a christian manner, and fulfil what the law required of me with respect to the marriage contract; which was agreeable to my own faith, and which I have performed according to the best of my understanding and conscience, although she or some of her accomplices have had the audacity to state in her petition to the Legislature, June session, 1818, that I advertised her by order of the society, adding that, "the poor misguided man has no will, and performs no act but through their influence." This, together with the whole of her petition and narrative, is a false and groundless imposition on the public, by which she has attempted to support numerous and criminal charges against the society, which never existed. And no wonder that she exclaimed in the Patriot of July last, that she did not know what evidence was necessary; for she made no use of the truth, but laid it entirely aside.[27]

It may be thought by some that many of these circumstances which I have related in the foregoing narrative concerning the said Mary, are trivial and too weak to merit any attention; but let it be considered that the seed of every tree in its germination is small, to whatever magnitude it may afterwards grow, and I have mentioned these things merely to shew the nature of her disposition, and that without an implicit obedience to her will, I never could enjoy any peace, and as her manner ever was to rule and govern me, so she has endeavored to set up her authority over the society called Shakers; and not only so, but even to trample on the sagacity of the legislature of this State, intimating that they were duped by the influence of the society, as may be seen in the New-Hampshire Patriot of July 14.

And notwithstanding her cause has been twice dismissed by the legislature, and I offered to settle with her on terms which their committee and even her own counsel acknowledged just and reasonable, yet she was not satisfied—but, as I am credibly informed, she has been from town to town and from one county to another, in order to furnish herself with more testimony from those who like, herself have left the society, on account of their own immoral conduct, although I would not be understood to impute this character to all who may have left this society. Thus she has been employed in this business from June last until sometime in the latter part of October; at which time she returned to Enfield, and I once more gave her information where I have provided a home for her.

It has been currently reported, especially of late, that Ann Lee, the head or first leader of this society, (commonly called Shakers) and her brother and others in company with them were, some years ago, at Concord and other places in this State, pretending great divination, telling fortunes, and swindling people out of their property, &c.[28]

That there was a woman of that name and description accompanied by others, at Concord, and other places, in or about the year 1767, is not to be disputed, as there are persons now in this society who have a competent knowledge of this company, having been defrauded by them. But Ann Lee, the first leader of this society, nor yet her brother William, never were within the State of New-Hampshire. Nor did they *ever arrive in America until late in the year 1774, at least seven years after those were seen at Concord;* all of which can be substantiated *by living witnesses* who not only accompanied them from England, but also for many years before they came to America, and *ever after until their decease.* See also the Introduction to a publication entitled, "Christ's Second Appearing."

The following are a few remarks on certain charges and false insinuations against me and my brethren called Shakers, exhibited to the public by Mary Dyer in a pamphlet bearing a very unjust and false title, wherein she has undertaken to palm her own base conduct on the guiltless in order to screen herself.[29]

The first accusation is, that "there had been some disagreeables by my husband's being unsteady and given sometimes to intoxication." *See her pamp. p. 3.*

As to being unsteady, I am willing to acknowledge that I was fond of high company and used to attend trooping, training, and other public days; and sometimes on such occasions spend more time and money than was wisdom: and sometimes in such cases get what was called high; but in not more than three or four instances in all my life did I ever degrade myself in the eyes of the world by intoxication; and this I do not justify, but condemn it in myself & for conscience's sake have abandoned all such practices. But as this was a fault which I had before I ever saw the Shakers, and have since forsaken it, Mary must be greatly mistaken as to their making me worse instead of better for she has stated under oath that once I was one of the best of husbands, and that she believed I should have continued so had it not been for the Shakers.

2d. "It was distressing to have that union broke which we had heretofore supported." *See her pamp. p. 4.* —As if the Shakers had been disturbers of our peace. This insinuation is absolutely false, and clad with a mask of hypocrisy and deceit, as I have stated by her own confession that her affections were wholly withdrawn from me and placed on another nearly three years previous to this period. Therefore the attempt to palm this on the innocent is a deceptive trick of her's to impute her own faults to others.

3rd. "I offered to live with him as a slave." *See her pamp. p. 4.* True, but I did not wish for a slave. She would not live with me as a wife—she declared that she would sooner die. This may plainly show that she would rather be a slave to her own will than be a wife and show obedience to her husband. See also her note page 4th, where she says, "I have since heard him say he treated me so at that time, he thought I should come to some untimely end." This is genuine hypocrisy with which her fallacious disposition is replete. It is true, about the time I endeavored to prevail with her to abandon the faith of the Shakers and live with me as a wife and be obedient, as the law required. This put her into such a rage that I told her she need not comply; for seeing the passion she was in on this account, I was actually afraid she would put a period to her life. But how deceitfully and falsely she has changed sides—as if I then professed faith with the Shakers, and was distressing her on that account, when in truth it was directly the reverse! However this is no more false than most of her other charges.

4th. "He said I should go out of his family if I did not renounce my belief in the Shakers." See her pam. p. 4.—That I desired her to go among the Shakers is true, being weary of her incessant clamor and argumentation in favor of their religious faith: but as this was when my mind was not with them, it can be no ground of accusation against any but ourselves. Why does she ascribe our faults to the innocent? The Shakers never came after us, but we went after them.

5th. "In the month of August we mutually gave up the idea of being Shakers and became harmonious." Also "In February, 1812," she states that I "called on the Shakers in Alfred, and returned home strong in the belief that they were the only true church." "We wrote them a friendly letter," &c. See her pamp. p. 5.

Answer. With regard to this first assertion, that "we mutually gave up the idea of being Shakers," it may be seen according to her own statement that I had abandoned my faith and profession with the Shakers before that time: but to obviate this matter more clearly I will here insert a short extract from that friendly letter of which she speaks, as that, perhaps, may be the most credible evidence, viz. "My husband tried to overcome me and bring me into the things of the flesh; but I told him would die before I would renounce my faith with the Shakers;" also much more to the same effect.

Had Mary Dyer inserted this and other contents of the aforesaid letter, and others of her own composition and signature, they would have given a very different idea to the reader, and a very different aspect to her pamphlet throughout—they would have shown with what extreme joy she was filled when I was returned home to think I had received the same faith to travail with her—they would have shown in many instances her solicitations to the Shakers, requesting them to take her children, assigning reasons for her importunities, viz. That Betsey had arrived to that age, that she would be likely attracted to the fashions of the world; and that Orville, being of a disposition similar to herself and not willing to be dictated by his older brother, was liable to be ruined, &c. These things she labored hard to impress on their minds: also, in September the same year, when some of them were at Stewartstown, she repeated the same solicitations and further said, that she believed that God had sent them there with a waggon, that they might convey the children to Enfield; insomuch that it was with difficulty that she was denied. Mary Dyer has not forgotten these things, although so long drunk with malice and passion. She may quibble and deny them as she is wont to do, but they are notorious and have been proved not only by her own written acknowledgment, but also fully substantiated by other competent evidence. And the only way we became harmonious was, I let her do just as she pleased; and in this way I could possibly live with her and in no other.

6th. "That when he returned from Connecticut he brought orders from the Shaker elders for me to go there immediately with my other children, and they would provide for us a house and other necessaries to make the family comfortable." *See her pamp. p. 5.*

Answer. The whole of this statement is false. The elders never sent any such word, nor did ever I tell her so. She went freely of choice, which I can prove by Daniel Taylor and Sarah Curtis, who went with her at that time to see the Shakers.

7th. She says that "the elders talked ridiculously to me because I was unreconciled and came filled with my natural and carnal affections, &c." *See her pamp. p. 6.*

Answer. To use her own expression, let Mary Dyer come out from be-hind the veil and own her filthy conduct and not try to palm her own evil on the elders; let her tell mankind what those natural and carnal affections were; had she told them that she came with her natural affec-tions withdrawn from her husband and vilely placed on another man of the society called Shakers, as before stated, the public would have seen the deception of the narrative. The truth is—what caused her great dis-tress at that and all other times was, she tried to daub it over with some-thing to make it appear spiritual, which she could not do; but because the elders would not acquiesce in her fleshly sense and licentious system, she has deceitfully endeavored to throw back her foul character upon the innocent; and as she has undertaken to disclose to the world the immorality of the people called Shakers, if she will take to herself what belongs to her, the public will find the people to be what they profess and she will be left to reap the fruit of her own vile conduct.

8th. She states that her children and furniture were distributed in the different families. *See her pamp. p. 7.*

Answer. True, agreeable to her desire, some of the children were placed in another family about 60 rods distant, where they could be much more comfortably taken care of and provided for than what they could be to remain all together. As to the furniture, we mutually lent about fifty dollars worth to a poor family from Stewartstown who professed faith with us. We did this as a deed of charity, expecting at the same time the articles would be consumed among them. Mary need not lay this charge to the Shakers; we voluntarily performed the act ourselves. And will she take back her hand from this deed of charity? But we should not have been able to have performed this deed had we not been furnished by others.

9th. That there appeared to be a man selected out, who was filled with the spirit of earth. *See her pamp. p. 8.*

Answer. I do not know of any definite meaning to the phrase *spirit of earth,* (except it means saltpeter) it would therefore seem proper to ask Mary some questions on the subject before I can fully elucidate the charge. Firstly, was this the man who stood in care with elder Edmund Lougee? Was it he to whom you manifested such peculiar love and union, and through whom, as you said, you received Christ? Was it the man on whom your eyes were cast from day to day with looks and gestures of wantonness? even he to whom that honor belongs, which you have ascribed to yourself, that of eluding your snares and keeping at a distance? If you answer these questions in the affirmative, I will proceed. As I have had ten times the opportunity to know the order of the family in which Mary lived, and also the people at large with whom I stand connected, I testify that her statements and insinuations concerning them are totally false—that they disapprove and disallow both by word and practice, all connexions, doctrines and ill treatment, of which they are accused through the tongue of malice by a censorious woman. It is remarkable that in the above charge, as well as in most if not all, others exhibited by Mary Dyer against the Shakers, she has portrayed her own real character distinctly from any other within my knowledge. For she had promptly told me of two men to whom she felt her union and affections before ever she came to the Shakers; and not only so, but had abundantly proved it by her conduct as before stated.[30]

10th. "I then questioned some of the lower order about these things and they acquainted the elders of it, and I was called to an account for it," &c. *See her pamp. p. 9.*

Answer. After Mary had tried in vain to dupe the ministry and elders to establish her licentious plan, which she calls spiritual marriage, she tried to insinuate it into others in a deceptious manner. But she was told by the elders, if she did not desist from such proceedings, they would expose her publicly. Had she stated in her pamphlet what it was that she questioned some of the lower order about, (as she is pleased to call them) it would have left the matter in the light; but as she has not, I shall only refer the reader to Sarah Curtis' affidavit, where it can be easily seen in what a deceitful manner and in what a false color she made all these statements.

11th. "Then they suffered me to have more privilege with my children for a short time, then they took them all from me. Twice they were so sick their lives were despaired of," &c. *See her pamp. p. 10.*

Answer. These statements are groundless falsehoods. Firstly, she had the care of her children, to instruct them (particularly the youngest) and all other care that is necessary for a mother to take of her children, especially when they were unwell, until a few days before she left the society; at which time I discovered that her management was very injurious to them; for she would teach them to use deceit to cover her faults as well as their own. I then desired the overseers to take them under their protection according to their agreement. This I did conscientiously for their safety. Secondly, the children never were so sick at any time as to be confined to the house while she was with the society, excepting when they had the measles. The two youngest had them when she was gone a journey to Stewartstown; the others she assisted in taking the care of herself. *See Lucy Lyon's affidavit.*

12th. "The father and mother came to see me," and said, "what liberty we give you, you may improve and it is no sin," &c. *See her pamph.*

Answer. By this charge it seems she would endeavor to insinuate into the minds of the public, that they gave her liberty to commit some gross evils, but she has not mentioned anything that she was tolerated in that was evil. If they had indulged her in the gratification of her licentious desires and permitted her to propagate the same, I presume she never would have let loose her slanderous tongue against them; but the truth is, they never gave her nor any other persons, liberty to violate any existing law either of God or man; neither can she prove any of those charges under that color in which she has represented them.

13th. "One of the elders said I must endure a certain scene to prepare me for their holy state, but he did not know I should be able to endure it and live," &c. *See her pamp. p. 11.*

Answer. Whether any elder ever told her so or not; I know not, but if he was not sensible that she needed to go through a scene of mortification to her own evil propensities, in order to bring her to anything virtuous, I was: but in this statement she has been very careful not to name the elder, nor the torture which he prepared for her to pass through. Therefore, as I am well acquainted with her disposition, I must suppose that if any elder had told her that she must submit herself to any good order which might be established for the good of society, such as to do justly, live uprightly, and not spend her time idly, in tattling and mischief making, it would be the greatest torture that could be inflicted on her. This will appear evident if the reader will only advert to her pamphlet, page 17, where she says, "I asked him to finish my days," which was for no other reason than my requesting her to go with me about 60 rods, to where I had made a comfortable provision for her entertainment.

14th. "They become so bold I was obliged to defend myself," &c.

Answer. This charge was investigated by a committee appointed by the Legislature of June last; and this boldness proved to be, that Moses Jewett[31] came into the room where she was sweeping and turned about and went out without offering to touch or molest her in the least, or even speaking a word. This is just like all the rest of her slanderous accusations: only take away the color and there is nothing left.

15th. "I frequently asked the privilege of taking a journey to go to my friends—they would not suffer it; neither would they let me send a letter, nor receive one, unless they first examined it. They forbid my opening any letter until they had seen it," &c.

Answer. All these statements are without the least color of truth. Once or twice she mentioned to me that she should be glad to go off an hundred miles or more; but this she intimated, was for the purpose of preaching the doctrine of the Shakers; I told her that we had better be steady and go to work and free ourselves from embarrassment, for I thought we had been burden and expense enough to the society, without their having to fix her out for preaching, while she behaved so unbecomingly at home. It was I and not the Shakers that prohibited her. I had too much regard for justice and truth to apply to the society for assistance and have her riding about at their expense. As to the other charges, she nor I never were prohibited from writing and sending letters, when and where we pleased, nor was there any compulsion in the case by any of the society. I have frequently received letters and never knew an elder or any body else to open or break a seal of any letter directed to me or any other person.

16th. "They did not afford me medical aid," &c.

Answer. She never was so unwell but what she was able to be about the house, which rendered it unnecessary to call upon the physicians: but had I or any other person attempted it, it would have been of no use; for she was so tenacious of her own skill, that for years before we came among this people, she was opposed to having any medical assistance called for on any occasion. She had liberty to apply for anything for her health while in this society, and was in much better circumstances on this account than ever she was before, while living with me. This is one of her false imputations to insinuate something against the society.

17th. "The elders charged me not to expose their practices, for it was a secret, and the world never did know it nor never was to; and if I told it they would deny it and make me the liar," &c. *See her pamp. p. 18.*

Answer. The elders never told Mary Dyer not to publish what they did do but told her not to report what they did not do. After she had done all that she could to set up her plan of spiritual marriage, and could get no one to join with her; and being filled with malice, she went to some of the elders and falsely asserted: "This is your faith, and you need not deny it." But they told her they had no such faith, and if she spread any such report, they should continue to deny it, and it would make her the liar. See Lucy Lyon's affidavit. This is one of her lying accusations. The truth is, they never told her not to expose their practices, but told her not to report her own debauched stuff as their faith; but this she has done to palm her own evil practices on the society.

18th. "He said, it appeared to him sometimes as tho' he should die, to treat me as he was obliged to," &c. *See her pamp. p. 14.*

Answer. I never said so: and if I ever said any thing that *resembled it in the least*, it was in consequence of her ill conduct: but the charge seems to be calculated to impose upon mankind the idea, that the people called Shakers obliged me to treat her in an abusive manner, when the truth is, they never did; for they always advised me to treat her in a Christian manner, which I have always done according to the best of my understanding, and feel justified in the sight of God and all men: which will be granted by the candid, who are acquainted with my dealing with her. I feel conscious that I have borne with her as far as any man would, in similar circumstances. Therefore, her statement is merely a false insinuation.

19th. "The next morning, they sent my husband twenty-eight miles to hire my board," &c. *See her pamp. p. 15.*

Answer. This is entirely misrepresented; for it was my own calculation. The elders and people never undertook to dictate me, as to what way and where I should provide for my wife. But her envy is against the society collectively, and not against me individually, therefore her scheme was to come among the people, and behave in such a base manner, as to oblige me to do something that she could deceitfully call abuse, and then go away and report what the *Shakers* had done to her as though I *was Shakers*, in the plural.

20th. "At length my husband entered the room in a passion, seized me in order to thrust me out of the door"; —"tore my clothes very badly. They clenched hold of my feet with my clothes and dragged me out of the door, down four steps to the ground; then into the street," &c. *See her pamp. p. 16.*

Answer. These charges are colored and mutilated in the extreme, in order to excite the feelings of the ignorant and to raise an enmity against the society, to which I belong; but had she stated all the occurrences of this transaction as they were, and stated the whole of her imperious language and conduct, there is no candid person but what would say that I used as much lenity as ought to be shown to such a person, in taking her up carefully without hurting or injuring her in the least, and carrying her to a comfortable place; where her clamor and noise would not disturb a family of between thirty and forty persons. But as she came to seek an occasion; she has been driven to the necessity to report untruths to deceive people that are not Shakers (as she expresses it,)—but for the particulars of this transaction, I refer the reader to the foregoing candid statement.

21st. "Now though all are in trouble, none know of any but their own." *See her pam. p. 18.*

Answer. If this statement of Mary Dyer's be true, that none know of any but their own, how came she to find it out?

The following charges of the said Mary, I observed exhibited in the New-Hampshire Patriot of July 14, 1818: published by request.

Where she begins with loud and indefinite hints as though there was some horrible impiety and oppression existing somewhere, the proof of which is her mere assertion.

The first definite charge she has brought against the Shakers, is the horrid crime of civility, by which (as she would have it,) they influenced the minds of the people, by inviting the members to a full examination of those things whereof she had accused them. In this it appears that she would endeavor to show the public, that the Legislature was formed of dupes: and that their honorable committee was incapable of judging of facts without the assistance of her slanderous tongue. But had her friends told her that hints and bare assertions were not proper evidence to legislate from, and that the truth was the only evidence necessary, perhaps she would not have appeared before the Legislature with a cause that would not bear examination.

2. "You hold that no untruth is a lie to your God that upholdeth the Shakers; it is only deceiving satan and his kingdom, meaning people that are not Shakers, &c."

Answer. This cannot be true, for they hold that there is no difference in speaking the truth, whether to a good man or a bad man; truth is truth, and a lie is a lie, wherever it is spoken. They hold, the only way to deceive Satan is, to speak the truth and walk in it. I conceive that the definite signification of satan is adversary, and perhaps the reason that the adversary got so deceived in what he expected to obtain by the Legislature last session was that the Shakers appeared with the truth, and nothing but the truth. Had they appeared with lies, deceit and quibbling, the committee no doubt would have detected them, and they would have been left to exclaim, "We did not know what evidence was necessary."

3. "You know that I was locked in this house a number of times by some person, and I never had the key at any time," &c.

Answer. These statements are not true; for there were two outside doors to the hall that led to her apartment, one of which was fastened inside by a button over the latch, which she could turn and go out and in at her pleasure: the other, whenever it was locked the key was left at her command.

4. She wishes to know what the Shakers call a civil manner of visiting children, &c.

Answer. Directly contrary to the manner that Mary has practiced in visiting ours, which has generally been to bring company with her, whom she knew to be prejudiced against the people, and introduce herself by defaming and scandalizing me and the society, and trying to inculcate disaffection and discontentment in the minds of the children.

This I call a very uncivil manner of visiting children.

5. "As to the property, the best part of it is secluded among the Shakers in deception," &c.

Answer. This has no color of truth, for I can prove by the appraisal bill of our personal property, and other records, that I have paid out for her support and to discharge other debts of our mutual contracting, at least an hundred dollars more than the value of what we brought to Enfield.[32] And the rest of our property consists in land, mostly wild, lying in Stewartstown, the deeds of which I still hold, having never parted with my title to the same.

6. "The writing I signed was no bond, neither were all my children's names to it," &c.

Answer. I refer the reader to her pamphlet, page 9th, where she says, they drew a bond which they intended should debar me and my husband from ever taking them again. She also says, I refused to sign the bond; here are two assertions of her's, one says they drew a bond and I refused to sign the bond; in the other, she says it is no bond. The reader is at his liberty to call which a *lie* he chooses, as they cannot *both be true.*

I consider it not only tedious, but unnecessary to notice all the deceitful hints and false coloring of this extraordinary woman, as they are too weak, insipid and contradictory to merit any attention. But as the foregoing are a few of the most prominent charges, contained in her pamphlet, calculated to convey ideas of criminality, all of which originated in malice and have been proved false—let it suffice the reader to consider that nothing true can be built on a false foundation.

A few observations on the testimony which the aforesaid Mary Dyer has procured, both in favor of her own character and also in support of her *charges against the Shakers*. By a slight examination, it will be seen by every candid person, that the testimony which the said Mary has affixed to her pamphlet, proves but very few, if any of her assertions, although it has been the means by which many well disposed people have considered some of her charges the truth; because something sworn to is affixed to her narrative, without examining whether it proves her statements true or not. But to the candid, the following remarks will show the validity of the testimony which she has produced.

Firstly. Although she has procured a number of certificates (perhaps from respectable people,) to substantiate her own character, yet all this is but negative testimony, for they can only state, that they did not know but what her character was good, or at most, that they considered it as such: this does not prove that she ever did, or does live a life of morality: and if she had lived a virtuous life previous to her coming among the Shakers, this does not prove that she did afterwards. There may be thousands who could state, that they knew nothing about her, or that they considered her to be a pious woman. There might have been as good testimony as this to prove the character of Benedict Arnold good, prior to his malconduct at West Point.[33] It was there that he betrayed his trust, lost his honor, and made his base character notorious. But I think I have had as good an opportunity to become acquainted with Mary Dyer's character and conduct, as any other person; which for the honor of my family I ever kept concealed as far as possible, until she made herself conspicuous.

Secondly. Concerning the validity of the affidavits she has produced.

Jeremiah and Deborah Towle, in their testimony were able to state a number of things which the said Mary had told them, but could not say whether she told the truth or not. Next they state something as though I abused her at the time I pursued her and brought back the child: this does not prove any of her charges against the Shakers, it comes against me individually; but she has not accused *me of it.*

Calvin Eaton of Hanover, testifies much what she and her associates told him, and has affirmed to the same; but cannot tell whether they told him the truth or not: all of which proves nothing that she has charged against the Shakers.

Moody Rich of Maidstone, Vt. tells you that he went in company with her to Enfield, and endeavored to prevail on me to let her see and converse with her children, but was unsuccessful—also states that they, (the Shakers,) would not suffer her to converse with her children, even in their presence; both of which statements I am fully prepared to prove false. And further he states, that he has since conversed with me, and has stated a number of things, (perhaps as true as the other before mentioned,) in a highly colored style, all of which prove nothing against the Shakers; as I was an hundred miles from any of them, and acted wholly from my own principle.

John Williams of Hanover, makes out that Mary Dyer told him that there was licentiousness among the Shakers. No doubt she has told a thousand others the same: but this testimony does not prove that she told him the truth.

Daniel Pettee and Moses Jones, have testified to something which they say was transacted among the Shakers when they were with them, which must have been transacted between thirty and forty years ago. This, Mary has collected to prove numerous charges, which she says were transacted between the years, 1811 and 1816; but I can find no person in this society who has the least knowledge of any such transactions as they have stated.

Lastly. A few observations on those quotations of Mary Dyer, on the Shakers' publication, entitled *Christ's Second Appearing.*

It is notorious that Mary Dyer in her pamphlet strenuously insists, that the Shakers hold to a spiritual marriage, as tho' there was something in it very criminal.—But what is it? True, they, according to the apostle's term, profess to be joined or married to Christ in the same Spirit by which he was united to God, and they, by bearing his cross against all sin, against all corporal and fleshly gratifications whatever, and against all carnal or fleshly desires and conceptions of the mind—walk even as he walked, and become united with him in the same Spirit. This and this only is what they call a spiritual marriage, or being joined to the Lord in one Spirit. And this is the only means of purification ever taught or practiced by Christ and his Apostles, or by the Shakers to obtain a spiritual marriage, or to be united to God. Nor has Mary Dyer proved anything to the contrary by all her assertions, false coloring, and concupiscent hints, either by her quotations from the Shakers' publication, entitled *Christ's Second Appearing*, or in any other way. But as the said Mary's insignificant statements on this subject, are too vague and disgusting to merit any investigation, I shall only refer the reader to the aforesaid publication, where the matter may be seen stated in its true and proper light, wholly independent of her lascivious and false comments, and by which it may be seen that she, like *Celsus the Epicurean*, has changed the truth into a LIE, and the doctrine of Jesus Christ into lasciviousness.[34] As saith Jude, "There should be mockers in the last time, who should walk after their own ungodly lusts. These be they who separate themselves, sensual having not the Spirit."[35]

JOSEPH DYER.

The following is a copy of a letter from JOSEPH *to* MARY DYER.[36]
Enfield, Nov. 5, 1818.

"MARY,

As I conceive you do not consider what you are doing in relation to our property, I write the following to inform you what you have already done towards spending what little property we had. Firstly, you well know that you have twice made application to the legislature for their interference to deprive me of my right of government, as the man or first agent of the family—an inherent right granted me not only by the Almighty, but granted and guaranteed also by the Constitution and laws both of the United States and this State. This you have endeavored to obtain in a deceptious manner, by trying to criminate the society of which I am a member; by your false insinuations, that under the pretence of criminating the Shakers to obtain the aid of the Legislature to deprive me of that which every candid man will consider next to life; for, take away his right of government, which will render him an outlaw, and what has he left? This you have done for no other cause than barely on the account of my religious faith; but I shall not voluntarily surrender the rights and privileges with which I am vested: therefore you have brought me to the necessity of defending myself against your malicious slander. Twice I have been brought to the necessity of meeting your groundless charges before the legislature, which were attended with heavy bills of cost on me; to defray which I have sold one lot of land in Stewartstown and applied part of the proceeds to that purpose; and not only this, but various other expences, not yet considered, which will amount to no small sum. These expenses and costs, added to one hundred and twenty-four dollars and eighty cents, which I have paid for your support, are not inconsiderable when compared with our property; but I can inform you, if such expenditures do not cease, our property will soon be gone. But you may say it is against the Shakers, because they will not give up the children to you, and I need not defend; but depriving me of my government is against myself, and I shall defend my rights to the last cent of our property if occasion requires. As you and your associates have said much against the Shakers for not giving the children to you, when they, at the same time, are bound by their covenant to us to protect them and bring them up according to their faith; and we, on our part, have bound ourselves by our covenant not to molest or trouble them on the account of our children. But perhaps you will say you do not hold them to their covenant; but I do, and consider them holden by solemn covenant to fulfil their duty to the children according to the stipulations, and also, I hold myself bound by the same stipulations, not to molest or trouble them nor suffer it to be done by any under my care; and this I shall do so long as I am the first agent. I consider myself bound by law and justice, to indemnify them for all cost and expenses arising from any breach of these stipulations, and this I shall do so long as I have it in my power, and property left to do it; therefore they have no right to give the children up to any other but me, nor is there any just cause that they should be put to any cost on their account. But you and your associates may think that these expenses are coming out of the Shakers: you are mistaken; you will find it comes out of our property."

POETRY.[37]

1. Go search the whole creation,
   And trace the world around,
   See if in any nation,
   A people can be found,
   Whose doctrine and behaviour
   Is honest just and true,
   Who live like Christ the Saviour;
   Who are the faithful few.

2. To draw the perfect likeness
   Of God's beloved few,
   With justness and exactness,
   Is more than I can do;
   But give me leave to mention
   Those virtues which excel,
   Which grace the new creation,
   Where God delights to dwell.

3. Upright in all their dealing,
   And just in every case,
   A friendly tender feeling
   For all the human race:
   They follow Christ's example,
   With all their heart and mind,
   Like children mild and simple,
   Long suff'ring, meek and kind.

4. In love they are united,
   They serve the Lord with zeal,
   While others are invited
   To share the bliss they feel:
   Their love cannot be mixed
   With that which leads to sin,
   Nor is it solely fixed
   On self's beloved kin.

5. An interest they inherit,
   That strangers do not find,
   A watchful prayerful spirit,
   A peaceful humble mind;
   A thankful heart possessing,
   To crosses reconcil'd,
   And this insures a blessing
   To every gospel child.

6. These are the heirs of heaven,
   And thither are they bound;
   The likeness here is given,
   The people can be found;
   With Christ they are partakers,
   Tho' form'd of flesh and blood,
   And you may call them Shakers,
   These people are of God.

⌐

A part of the testimony affixed to this narrative was taken from persons who belong to the society, and a part of from those who do not. But I am not unaware of the deceitful and malicious plan of the said Mary and her associates, in attempting to invalidate the testimony of those who are of this society, where her conduct is most notorious; on the basis that they are perfectly united in their religious principles, and that this constitutes them one; and therefore, their testimony is not to be credited. But let it be considered whether they are any more united than what our Saviour enjoined on his followers? and further, if this be a sufficient reason for rejecting their testimony, it lays each denomination of professed christians under the necessity of being at variance in their own churches, and differing one from another in their own sentiments of faith, in order to render any of their testimony valid. For with the same propriety all the testimony of the calvinistic order might be discredited, because they hold to predestination; or of the baptists, because they hold to immersion, and so of all other sects. But this scheme will appear contemptible and disgusting to every man of sense and candor; and was invented in order to evade the force of truth by those who have been infuriated with malice under a specious pretence that the Shakers are combined to secrete their own evils. But who says so? or what proof is there of this charge? And further I would ask the candid, which is entitled to the greatest credit, a person who will state a fact under oath at one time and contradict it at another, or a society who are unimpeached only by the tongue of slander?

———

[No. 1]

I, *Sarah Curtis*, of Braintree, Vt., of lawful age, testify and say, that about the year, 1809, or 10, I first became personally acquainted with Joseph and Mary Dyer, who frequently attended the Methodist meeting to which I belonged: sometimes they attended in Canaan where I resided, and sometimes in Stewartstown; at which meetings the said Mary manifested a strong desire to have the church privileges of the Methodist order; at the same time professing to belong to the Christian order so called, in which she was indulged for a time; but being unwilling to conform to their discipline, was denied the privileges that she desired in the Methodist order, which so irritated her that she made such disturbance that she was several times requested by the minister to take her seat and be peaceable or leave the room and let others enjoy their religious devotion, but she withdrew and made a great outcry. And further that during the latter part of the year 1811 it was the common report in our neighborhood that Joseph and Mary Dyer were Shakers – that in the year 1812 I became more acquainted with their profession, in which time she frequently used every argument and insinuation in her power to attract my mind to the Shakers' faith.

Furthermore, about the first of October of the same year I attended a meeting held by the Shaker Elders at Joseph Dyer's house, where I saw Mary Dyer dressed in shaker habit, and she appeared zealous in the approbation of their testimony, and used all her influence to persuade me and others present to join in the Shakers' faith, which induced me to tarry over night and enquire further into their faith and principles; during my stay the said Mary manifested a strong desire to be freed from the care of her children, and the burthen of her family; and exclaimed, O! Sarah, how I wish I was as free from bondage as you are; then turning to the Shaker Elders said, you have got to help me out of my bondage, to which one of them replied you have taken time to travel into your bondage, and you have got to take time to travel out again.

I further testify and say that about the first of January 1813, I went into the family of said Joseph and Mary Dyer at Stewartstown to live, where she continued to use arguments to persuade me into a belief of faith with her, and having received some faith I was induced to go to Enfield with her, who was then preparing to go and to carry three of her children with her, and seemed very much animated and satisfied in so doing, and manifested nothing to the contrary on this journey, neither in relation to these nor the other two children which were already there. And notwithstanding all that she has published concerning the ill treatment of the Shakers to her on this visit, she exerted all her influence to gather me and her sister Fanny (who came with us) into their faith; and during the whole of this visit she manifested great satisfaction both in relation to the Shakers' faith and their conduct towards us; and vindicated the same to other people on our return home as she had opportunity. I further say that soon after we returned home, she began to prepare to move to Enfield herself, which she was very much engaged in, and appeared so well satisfied with her children's being there, that she was very much pleased with the idea of carrying my little sister Miriam down with her when she moved and advised to the same, stating how well children were taken care of among the Shakers. She moved down and carried the above mentioned sister of mine in the month of February according to the best of my recollection; and during the whole acquaintance that I had with the said Mary at Stewartstown, she never manifested to me any dissatisfaction in relation to the Shakers' faith or conduct, but her conversation and conduct proved to the contrary as stated above, also by an expression she made to me after she had lived at Enfield more than a year in the following words: "I do not think that the Shakers were sensible how zealous I was in their faith when I came here."

I further depose and say, that in the month of November 1813, I moved to Enfield, into the family where Mary Dyer lived, where I became closely and intimately acquainted with her; being her chief com-

panion both at work and lodging, and had an equal privilege of information with her, and by our close connections I had a better opportunity
to discover her sense in regard to what she has palmed upon the Shakers
as their spiritual marriage. Within a few weeks she began the attempt to
inculcate into my mind the idea of a spiritual help meet as she was
pleased to term it, intimating that she supposed herself to be the one
designed for Moses Atwood; and endeavoring to prove to me by scripture the idea that this was the intent of God in the creation. This was a
new subject to me, neither did I at that time understand what she was
after: and as her sense was disapprobated by the Elders she strove to
screen herself from contempt by accusing others of the same. She asserted to the Elders that there was others possessed of the same sense.
They asked her who? she answered Sarah Curtis, and her union is with
Daniel Taylor.[38] The Elders told her they had not discovered any such
thing in me, but, said they, if it is so it is of the flesh, and we condemn
it as much in her as we do in you. Then the said Mary came to me and
asked me if I did not set more by the aforesaid Taylor then I did by Joseph Dyer or any of the rest of the brethren, (See page 9th in a pamphlet
entitled a brief statement of the sufferings of Mary Dyer.) I told her I did
not—I esteemed Joseph as a father on the account of his kindness to me
and my relations: then the said Mary told me that the Elders said that
my union to Daniel Taylor was a fleshly union. This dissimulation in her
excited in me some hard feelings against the Elders, and they discovering that my union was lessening, called upon me to know the cause:
when I related the foregoing statement of the said Mary, then the Elders
related to me the circumstance to my full satisfaction of their innocence, which exposed to me fully for the first time, her false sense and
separate union which she held to one of the brethren which I found by
observation to be John Lyon, by observing such like singularities, as that
she would frequently start from her work and run to the windows and
doors and look after him when he passed by, and jump out of her bed
when she heard the steps of a man in the hall—would run to the door
and peep out to see who it was, &c.

I further say, that the said Mary Dyer's conduct was so unseemly and
indecent, the particulars of which for the honour of our sex I forbear to
mention, but say that it was so disagreeable to me that I requested to be
released from the burthen of lodging with her, which was granted. And

further according to the knowledge I had of her and the Shakers, she has acted the part of Potiphar's wife, for she was the only person in which I ever saw any lewdness or wantonness either in male or female, while I was with them.[39]

I further testify, that from all the knowledge I obtained of the Shakers' management of children, that they are treated more kindly and with less severity than what is common for children to receive from their parents. Also I never saw any thing that was abusive to them while I was with the Shakers, and I think I had as good an opportunity to know if there was any abuse as Mary Dyer.

I further testify, that I continued with the Shakers about two months after Mary Dyer left them, and during my stay with them I was kindly treated; and I left them on account of some privileges which I thought I could better enjoy among other people.

SARAH CURTIS.

September 12, 1818.
Grafton, ss. Enfield, Sept. 12, 1818. Personally appearing the above named Sarah Curtis, and made solemn oath that the foregoing declaration by her subscribed, contains the truth, and nothing but the truth. Before me,

E. EVANS, *Jus. Peace.*

[No. 2]

I, *Susannah Curtis*, of lawful age, do depose and say, That in the year 1811, I lived in the family of Joseph Dyer, in Stewartstown, about four months; that in this time there was a man (who called himself a preacher) made it his home there.[40] I think he was a man of as unbecoming behavior as any one I ever saw; that I had not been there long before I was convinced that Joseph's woman Mary Dyer, and this man had unlawful connexions together; for often I knew them to be in a room by themselves, while Joseph was out to his work; that one time in particular they were in another room by themselves for nearly two hours, in which time the said Joseph Dyer her husband came to me and got the pails and went and milked the cows and did his chores after he had been all day at work: that at another time, Mary Dyer and the said preacher went out together into the back part of Canaan in Vermont a preaching, leaving her husband and children at home to go dirty and ragged; that in this manner they spent a great part of their time; and when she was at home her attention was mostly to this man while her husband was neglected. And further, that she made the said preacher some new clothes in the time abovementioned, and in all things the said Mary appeared to regard him more than she did her husband. I further depose and say, that during the time aforesaid the said preacher being about to go a journey, talked a while with the said Mary in the door yard, and when parting they kissed each others' hand—and from all the acquaintance I ever had with her afterward while living in Stewartstown, it appeared evident that her attachment to this man was greater than it was to her husband.

SUSANNAH CURTIS.

June 11, 1818.
Grafton, ss. Enfield, June 11, 1818. Personally appearing Susannah Curtis, subscriber to the foregoing affidavit, and made solemn affirmation that the same contains the truth and nothing but the truth.—Before me,

E. EVANS, *Jus. Peace.*

[No. 3]
I, *Moses Hodge,* of lawful age, testify and say, that I lived a neighbor to Joseph Dyer and his wife when they lived in Stewartstown, and frequently heard them converse about going to live with the Shakers, and I thought that Mary Dyer his wife was from all her conversation and appearance the most forward to break up the family, and to go and live with the Shakers; and I was at the house of said Dyer one morning, and saw Mary Dyer, Daniel Taylor, Sarah Curtis, and three of Mary Dyer's children, who were about to start on a journey to Enfield, to the Shakers and pay them a visit, and leave their children with them, as she the said Mary informed me; And I believe that she was the first cause of his mind being led to the Shakers.

MOSES HODGE.

Sworn to before JEREMIAH EAMES, Just. Peace.
May 25, 1818.

[No. 4]
I, *Esther Hodge,* of lawful age, testify and say, that I lived a neighbor to

Joseph Dyer and his wife, when they lived in Stewartstown, and frequently heard them both speak of their faith with the Shakers, and I thought that Mary Dyer from every appearance, appeared to be the most earnest to leave her neighbors and go and join the Shakers; and Mary Dyer told me that when she should get to the Shakers, she should be released from the trouble of her family, which the said Mary seemed to long to be released from and further said, the Shakers will bring our children up much better than we can: and I thought if she had been willing to live with her husband as other women did with theirs, that we should not have lost one of the best of neighbors: and the said Mary further told me she believed it was an awful sin for her to have children: and this she told me before ever she went to see the Shakers: She also told me that she hardly knew how to wait till she could get ready to go down and live with them, and when the said Joseph Dyer left this town we lost a good neighbor, and an useful member of society.

ESTHER HODGE.

Sworn to before JEREMIAH EAMES, Jus. Peace.
May 25, 1818.

[No. 5]

We, *Elisha Dyer* and *Lucy Dyer*, of lawful age testify and say, that we were well acquainted with Joseph Dyer and his wife, Mary Dyer, and they were often at our house in Stewartstown, after they had been to see the Shakers, and spoke much in their favor, and both of them seemed to be determined to go and live with them, and appeared to be well agreed in so doing. And we can testify that Mary Dyer said she wanted to get rid of the burthen of her family, and be released. And Mary Dyer shewed, by all her conduct, that she was forward in the thing; and it was common report among our neighbors that she was forward, and more zealous than her husband, and some said she was the means of his joining the Shakers; and when he left the town we lost a good neighbor and an useful member of society.

ELISHA DYER,
LUCY DYER.

Sworn to before JEREMIAH EAMES, Jus. Peace.
May 25, 1818.

[No. 6]

I, *Daniel Taylor*, of lawful age, do testify and say, that in the year 1811, I lived in Heriford, in the province of Lower Canada, was a neighbor to Joseph and Mary Dyer—that in the latter part of the year aforesaid, the said Mary Dyer made exertions to induce me to join the Society of Shakers, professing herself to be fully established in their principles; in which her husband was not until the next year. That in the year 1812, I moved into the house of the said Joseph and Mary Dyer, that I frequently heard her express her satisfaction in relation to the two children, which they had lately conveyed to the said Society; also, I frequently heard her express her desire to be there herself, and further, that in January 1813, by her solicitations, I was induced to go with her to see the said society at Enfield, to which she professed to belong; at which time she carried the other three of her children, which were the oldest and two youngest. Also, before we started and on our journey she manifested her great satisfaction in taking her children to the said society. And I further say, that from all the acquaintance I had with the said Mary, which was for a number of years, she manifested a strong desire to have the preeminence over her husband; and oftentimes he would condescend to her rather than make difficulty.

DANIEL TAYLOR.

June 1, 1818. Solemnly affirmed to, before
E. EVANS, Jus. Peace.

[No. 7]

I, *John Lyon*, of Enfield, county of Grafton and State of New-Hampshire, do depose and say, that in the month of July 1811, Mary Dyer came to Enfield in company with her husband Joseph Dyer, which was the first time I ever saw her; at which time I heard her say she received faith in our religious tenets, though more fully established in them about four weeks afterward, as I have frequently heard her state to myself and others since, even to the last of her residence with this Society. That about one year after she came again to Enfield accompanied by her husband who she said had turned from, but that she had continued stedfast in the faith; and that this had been the case for about a year: that she also added—where should we both have been now if I had done as you said, and obeyed my husband. Also, she stated in my presence at the same time, the offers which her husband made her if she would return back to her former way of living, which she said she utterly refused; for the Lord had shown to her plainly that it was the work of the devil to draw both of our souls into death. Also, during this visit I heard her solicit Edmund Lougee, the head of the family, to take her daughter Betsy under his protection; which request was not at that time granted. In the month of September, 1812, I went to Stewartstown, in company with Moses Jewett: while there the said Mary Dyer strongly urged us to take two of her children home with us: And was much more solicitous in the matter than her husband; but we declined. In November the same year her husband brought the two children above mentioned to Enfield: and in January following, the said Mary brought the other three herself which were the oldest and two youngest, stating at the same time, that she and her husband were both agreed in the matter, and desired us to take them under our care. And further, for about the term of ten months she frequently importuned us to take the children under our care by a written agreement. At one particular time she desired us to persuade her husband to bind them by an indenture, that in case he should leave the society we could hold them.

I further depose and say, that the said Mary Dyer frequently declared in my hearing that her natural ties to her husband were wholly dissolved. That instead thereof she manifested a strong attachment to another man of the society; that being taxed with the same in my presence, she tried to vindicate and adopt it as the true Christian system; but being told that it was contrary to our faith or any principle of christianity, she made an appeal for an interview with the ministry, who plainly told her in my hearing that they wholly disapproved of any such thing, nor was there any such thing or sense owned among the people. Also, that whoever conducted in that manner it would separate them from our society, and much more to the same purpose.

And further, that the said Mary much of the time while she was with us manifested a very immodest and unbecoming appearance, especially in presence of the male sex, of which she appeared very fond. At one certain time I was called as a witness by her husband who had found her fastened up in a room with a man that was a stranger to him, who was unwilling to tell either his business or his name, which the said Dyer earnestly requested; at which she was very much irritated, and expressed the most scandalous invectives against her husband and the society. I further depose and say, that being personally acquainted with most of the treatment respecting Mary Dyer while she was among the people, I have never seen any thing that an unprejudiced person would call abusive either on the part of the society or by her husband, likewise that I heard her say the day before she left the society that the people had always treated her with kindness, and she meant to treat them so; which was the last concern of the society with her respecting how the matters between her and her husband should be regulated, as I have often heard him told that we should not interfere in matters between him and his wife, but he must fulfil what the law required of him in the marriage contract; the day before she went away I heard her state in my presence and a number of others that she never had seen any evil thing in any one that was held in union by the Society. Also, about a year afterwards I heard her say in the presence of a number; being asked by her husband how she came to spread such scandalous reports when she knew there was no truth in them. She replied, I never did; and turned to Moody Rich of Vermont, said, you know Judge Rich, that I always told you that I did not believe they lived in any evil actions, but I told you it was in the spirit. Furthermore, about one year after she left the society (according to the best of my recollection) she came to Enfield in company with the aforesaid Moody Rich, who asked me if they could see Joseph Dyer's children; to which I answered we have no objection to people's seeing their relations among us provided they conduct in a civil manner; accordingly they were conducted to the family where the children lived; when they returned I asked the said Rich if they saw the children, who replied we did, also if they look as if they were abused or discontented; he said they looked very well and contented, much more so than he expected by what he had heard.

Enfield, June 11, 1818.
JOHN LYON.

Grafton, ss. June 11, 1818. Personally appearing John Lyon, subscriber to the foregoing affidavit, and makes solemn affirmation that it contains the truth, and nothing but the truth. Before me,

E. EVANS, Just. Peace.

[No. 8]

I, *William Brown*, of Enfield, county of Grafton and State of New-Hampshire, testify and say, that I was given to the people called Shakers by my father (my mother being dead) when I was in the ninth year of my age, and continued to live with them until I was in the nineteenth year of my age; that for the whole time I continued with them they treated me with all the care and tenderness I could wish, in sickness or in health; that during said term I have never known any children among them treated with cruelty or oppression, but entirely contrary thereunto; neither have I ever heard any children complain of ill treatment, as I now recollect, who were among the said Shakers. And further, from the time of my first living with them until I was fifteen years of age or more—myself and others of my age were always indulged to retire to rest when we chose and to rise in the morning at our pleasure, generally in the evening of the shortest days between the hours of seven and eight, and rise about six o'clock in the morning, when we were in health; that I left the said Shakers in April last of choice, and when I expressed my purpose of leaving them they made no objection, but gave their consent that I might go; that I now live in said Enfield with Capt. Jonathan Bosworth, and am in the nineteenth year of my age.

WILLIAM BROWN.
Enfield, June 1, 1818.

Grafton, ss. June 1, 1818. Personally appearing William Brown, made solemn affirmation that the foregoing affidavit by him subscribed contains the truth and nothing but the truth. – Before me,

E. EVANS, Jus. Peace.

[No. 9]

I, *Samuel Brownson*, of Norwich, in the county of Windsor, and state of Vermont, do testify and say, that I moved with my family to Enfield, in the state of New-Hampshire, in the year 1812, and lived in said town with the society of people called Shakers nearly two years, in which time I became well acquainted with their faith and practice; and having perused a pamphlet published by Mary Dyer respecting said Society, in which I find she has grossly misrepresented the faith and practice of said people, as to children being called up in the morning at half past three in the summer and half past four in the winter—there was no such practice among the people; for the stated time for grown people to rise was at half past four in the summer and six in the winter. I further state, that all abuse to children is contrary to the faith and practice of the people. I was knowing of their having a boy about seven years old of a rude disposition, which they found very difficult to govern except they used corporeal punishment, which, from all that I could discover, they were very adverse to. Accordingly, they delivered the boy to his father, who lived in the family with me; and, in order to govern him, his father thought proper to put him in the shop where I worked, to keep him separate from the other children, where he was treated kindly, and no abusive treatment towards him whatever. His father, finding it difficult to keep him from the other children whom he was liable to corrupt by his vile language and had behaviour, thought fit to bind him out; accordingly, put him to his uncle a man of the world. I can also truly state, that while I was a resident among the people, I discovered in them nothing that was licentious or obscene.

SAMUEL BROWNSON.

State of Vermont: Windsor county. Norwich, September 1, 1818. Personally appeared Samuel Brownson, signer to the above instrument, and solemnly affirmed that the same contained the truth and nothing but the truth. Before me,

PIERCE BURTON, Jus. Peace.

[No. 10]

I, *Mary Mills*, of lawful age, do depose and say, that in the year 1812, discovering a very vague expression in a letter from Mary Dyer, I afterwards personally desired her to explain her meaning, to which she was very reluctant indeed; at length she told me she felt a particular union to one certain man of the society, naming the person at the same time; I answered that such a sense or connexion was entirely contrary to our faith and every precept and principle of the gospel; and which if she did not abandon, would separate her from the people; and also much more to the same purport, but the said Mary appeared to continue determined to establish it in the society as agreeable to the true Christian system, and to vindicate it by trying to prove it by scripture a spiritual union; but being peremptorily opposed by me and others, she appealed to the ministry for its approbation, who told her in the presence of me and three others that they utterly disapproved of and condemned any such union or connexion, and also much more to the same purpose. I further depose and say, that the said Mary Dyer often manifested her desire and free choice in my presence to secure her children to the society. And further, that when the said Mary was about to leave the society, she stated in the presence of me and another, that she could go without any embarrassment if it was not for one thing, which is (said she) that I have testified in public that I knew this to be the way of God, but now *I do not know how to turn it.* Also soon after I heard her say in presence of four others that she had never seen any evil thing in any one that was held in union in the society; but that they always treated her kindly, and that she meant to treat them in like manner; but (continued she) the reason why I go away is because the spirit I possess is opposite to the spirit you possess.

MARY MILLS.

June 1, 1818.

Grafton, ss. Enfield, June 1, 1818. Personally appearing the above named Mary Mills, subscriber to the foregoing affidavit, made solemn affirmation that the same contains the truth and nothing but the truth—Before me,

E. EVANS, Jus. Peace.

[No. 11]

I, *Lucy Lyon,* of lawful age, depose and say, that I became fully acquainted with Mary Dyer, by living in the family with her: and that I often heard her say, that if she had not been stronger in the faith of the Shakers than Joseph Dyer that their family would not have been among them; for (said she) after we came to Enfield the first time, Joseph tried to overcome me and make me live with him after the order of the world; but I told him I would not. Likewise I often heard her say that she had no more regard for Joseph Dyer, than for any other man, and that this had been the case with her for nearly three years prior to her coming to Enfield.

I further testify, that she told me that she had had an extraordinary attachment to Benjamin Putnam, a christian preacher, and also told what a pretty black-eyed man he was, and how delighted she was in his company. She further said, when she found he was going to get him a wife, it struck her to the heart, and after he got married he was dead to her.

I further depose and say, that about the last of November, 1812, we received a letter, date of the same month, containing some strange ideas which were very repugnant to our faith and principles, being covered with as much duplicity as it could be and reveal any thing; but from what we could discover of her ideas they were principles of obscenity communicated in a very blind manner to evade our understandings, as she afterwards stated that she did not intend we should understand them. The next time she came to Enfield, Jan. 24, 1813, in company with Daniel Taylor and Sarah Curtis and her sister Fanny, she brought three of her children with her; then she was requested to reveal those dark statements of the above mentioned letter, when she stated (though reluctantly) that she had a particular attachment to John Lyon, a member of our society. This investigation was first entered into between her and Mary Mills; but the said Mary Dyer being very much agitated with the idea of having her favorite principle condemned as sinful, unlawful, and unchaste, she strove to screen herself from contempt in the presence of those she terms Elders, where the above statements were rehearsed over in my presence, which she strove to cover over in a deceptious manner by calling it a spiritual union. The Elders told her that her calling it a spiritual union did not make it any better; it was the same principle of licentiousness that was practiced in the world among the dissolute. They also told her that there was not any such faith or sense owned in our society, and that whoever possessed that spiritual union that existed between the members of the Church of Christ, hated every fleshly desire. They also told her if she did not forsake such unchaste connections it would end in lewdness. This greatly irritated her. *See her pamphlet entitled "the Sufferings of Mary Dyer," page 6.* And further, I heard the elders reason with her upon the impropriety of her coming an hundred and thirty or forty miles and bringing others with her to be instructed into our faith and at the same time try to maintain such pernicious principles as the above.

I further testify and say, that on or about the 26th of February the said Mary Dyer moved into our family at Enfield; that she still maintained her attachment to the aforesaid John Lyon; that she often told me that from the first time she ever saw him her feelings were attached to him; and that he seemed the nearest to her of any person on earth. I have often seen her start from her work and run to the windows, look and gaze after him as he passed by; and frequently run from her shop to the house to

meet him as he went in. Also, her conversation comported with her conduct. She told me when she got a chance to speak to him it gave her great
satisfaction, and said if we did not let her union alone she should die.
Notwithstanding all that could be said or done to convince her that such
a spiritual union as she was trying to support was nothing better than
wantonness; yet she was determined to support it in opposition to our
faith; and went on trying to mate out the whole society. She selected out
a man for me, and told me that I had a particular union to him, and that
I need not deny it. I told her that there was no such thing – it was as far
from me as any thing in the heart of the earth; and that I had no fellowship with any such union. And the said Mary, finding no one that would
unite with her in her debauched sense among us, appealed to the ministry, and said that if we would not own it as that spiritual union spoken of
by the apostles, they would; which request was granted,—when they told
her that such a union had no relation to that spiritual marriage, which
was to be joined to the Lord in one spirit; that it was nothing more than
that union which joined man and woman together, and made of them
twain one flesh, and utterly condemned it as corrupt, and told her if she
did not abandon such things it would separate her from this people.

I further say that Mary Dyer came to Mary Mills and me before she left
our family and said, "this spiritual marriage is your faith and you need not
deny it." But we told we had no such faith, and if she spread any such report we should continue to deny it, and it would make her a liar for there
was no such thing existing among us. And further, the said Mary is the
only person I ever knew who undertook to couple out the members of our
society, a male and a female, calling it a spiritual marriage, which sense
was utterly condemned in my presence by the ministry, elders and people.
I further testify, that during the time of her residence among us she tried
to form an intimate connection with me and told me many things, which
were fabricated from her own imagination, very absurd and disgusting;
and which I conceive too indecent to mention; some of which I have lately heard by some of our neighbors in the same expressions which she made
to me, which she has thrown back and palmed upon the Shakers.[41]

I further say, that she is the only person that I ever knew who had
such filthy imaginations, which she has undertaken to support as being
our faith and practice; but we often told her we had no fellowship with
the unfruitful works of darkness—that if people had not that faith to

take their cross and deny themselves every fleshly desire, they had better live in a lawful married state.

I further depose and say, that I lived in the family where Joseph Dyer lived at the time the said Mary tendered herself upon her husband's advertisement, and was knowing to his letting her have of the best of their furniture to the amount of fifty dollars at her own appraisal. And further the said Joseph requested me to wait on her, if she needed any thing to make her comfortable in case of his absence. This continued two or three days, at which time I heard Joseph request her to go to the dining-room of the family and eat her victuals; but she showed some reluctance, saying, "The more I keep separate from the family the better I feel;" yet she complied with his request. And further, that I had no care of her work more nor less, and had no concern with her in any thing only for the two or three days before mentioned. Also, that I am the only person that had any concern with her of our society in my knowledge, excepting her husband. I further say, that having the care of the rest of the building in which she resided, I was knowing to the fastening of the doors, and say that she could not be locked in with the fastenings that were on the doors when she was here; for there were two outer doors belonging to the hall leading to her apartment, and only one lock; the other door was fastened by a button over the latch, which she could turn and go out at her pleasure.

I further testify, that I was knowing to all the sickness that Joseph and Mary Dyer's children had while the said Mary resided in our society, which was as follows: Marshall and Betsey had the measles in the family where Mary lived, and she and I took care of them together. Orville who lived in the same family was accidentally scalded. Mary instantly assisted in taking care of him; and Joseph, jr. had a sore on his arm, also he accidentally got his hand cut and had a weak turn—and she took the whole care of him. And further, Jerrub and Joseph, jr. the two youngest, had the measles soon after she brought them to Enfield, at which time she was gone to Stewartstown, and before she returned they got well. This is the only sickness that they had while she was with us, excepting some colds. I further say that she was never prohibited from seeing or inquiring after them when she was pleased while she lived in our society.

Enfield, Sept. 19, 1818.
LUCY LYON.

[No. 12]

I, *Lovicy Childs*, of lawful age, depose and say, that I lived in a small family where Mary Dyer frequently visited while living among the society called Shakers at Enfield, that she in her visits was very officious in trying to inculcate into me and others secretly principles of licentiousness as being acceptable in the sight of God; such as are contrary to the faith and practice of the society or any other people who regard chastity as a virtue. And further that in all her secret insinuations to me she manifested that wantonness which is degrading to the female character. And she is the only person in which I ever saw such wantonness, either in looks, speech or behavior among the society.

LOVICY CHILDS.

June 11, 1818.

Grafton, ss. June 11, 1818. Personally appearing the above named Lovicy Childs, subscriber to the above affidavit, made solemn affirmation that the same contains the truth and nothing but the truth.—before me,

E. EVANS, Jus. Peace.

[No. 13]

I *Mary O'Neil*, of lawful age, testify and say, that I lived with the Shakers about seven years, in that family where Mary Dyer lived while she was with them, where I became personally acquainted with her, and was intimately connected with her in work and other family concerns, during the whole time that she was with the Shakers—that from the first of her living with them, I often heard her express how glad she was that she had got released from the care of her family; so that she could be a free woman, and that I have frequently heard her say, that her husband seemed no nearer to her than any other man. I further testify that she frequently tried to inculcate into me the idea of a spiritual helpmeet, and often asked if I did not think the time would come, when every one would have a spiritual mate. I told her that I did not: then she would say, I do; for I believe there is somebody created for a mate to every one in the spirit. This kind of conversation was frequent during the greatest part of the time that she lived in the family. And further she would often tell me of particular persons, male and female, which she said were created for each other, and would be mated together; and would ask me if I did not think that there was a mate for me in the spirit, I told her that I did not, she said she did believe there was, for (said she) there is one created for you, and you will have a mate. And I further testify, that she often conversed with me about John Lyon, in the following manner: she would ask me if I did not think that there was a mate for him, and whether I thought he would have one: I told her that I did not believe any thing about such stuff, as I was satisfied it was directly contrary to the faith, precepts, and practice of the Shakers; but she said she did, and would ask me who I thought she had in view; I told her that I did not know her thoughts, though I was satisfied that she meant herself: then she would say that she believed that there was one for him, and we should all know who it was when Mary Mills (the head woman in the family) is out of the way. She would often say that she expected that John Lyon would be the head of the family; and by her frequent expressions she strongly intimated that she expected to be the head among the women. I further say, that her conduct was more conspicuous than her language, for I soon found by observation, that her attachment was to the aforesaid John Lyon: I observed that she would often put herself in a way to meet him, and would run to the windows and doors to see him as he passed by; and many times manifested a very wanton appearance. And I further state that the said Mary Dyer is the only person that I ever heard undertake to establish any such plan as to mate out the society, or any part of them a male and a female, or even to intimate any such thing was acceptable to God while I lived with the Shakers.

I further depose and say, that the said Mary Dyer often tried to instill into me principles of obscenity and lewdness, even to teach me such unseemly practices as modesty forbids to mention. See Romans 1 ch. 26 verse.[42] I further say that her unseemly insinuations were the cause of my leaving the Shakers: also I thought after I had received her pamphlet, that I should not think strange if she, on account of her own conduct, had been obliged to think of the first chapter of Romans the greatest part of the time. I further testify that I was present at the time that Joseph Dyer carried Mary, his wife, out of the house of Edmund Lougee, and that there was no such abuse offered in this transaction as she has stated in her pamphlet; but her husband took her up in his arms and carried her carefully out of the house and set her down on her feet, and

I did not see any part of her touch the floor, steps or ground, though she strove against him until she shook off her cap and shawl: and further— this transaction took place between 3 and 4 o'clock in a very warm afternoon—I saw the whole affair, and say that I saw no abuse on the part of her husband or any one of the Society.

MARY O'NEIL.
Nov. 14, 1818.

State of New-Hampshire, Nov. 14, 1818. Then personally appeared Mary O'Neil, and made solemn affirmation that the above declaration by her subscribed, contains the truth and nothing but the truth, before me, Edward Evans, Notary Public.

[No. 14]

I, *Abigail Mecham,* of lawful age, testify and say, that in the month of August or September, in the year eighteen hundred and fourteen, I was at the Shakers' meeting in Enfield, on the Sabbath; that I heard Mary Dyer say in public at said meeting that the people she was then with was the people of God, and that she knew them to be such; and that that was right, and that only; And that if she should leave the way that the fault would be her own. And that I also saw Mrs. Dyer in the spring of the year following at the house of Challis Currier, and in conversation with her heard her speak diminutively of the Shaker people that she had been with, and also charged them with immoral conduct; when I observed to her that her language was very different from what it was when I saw you at the Shakers' meeting—you then said that they were the only people of God: and her reply was that "it was some other person or woman that spoke, and not me, for I never spoke in their meeting after the first year that I lived with them."

ABIGAIL MECHAM.

State of New-Hampshire – Grafton, ss. Enfield, January 15, 1818. Personally appeared Abigail Mecham and subscribed to the above statements, and made solemn oath that the same contained the truth and nothing but the truth, before me,

GEORGE CONANT, Jus. Peace.

[No. 15]

I, *Betsy Foster*, of Canterbury, in the county of Rockingham, and State of New-Hampshire, do depose and say, that for more than twenty years last past, I have lived in the vicinity of the people called Shakers in said town of Canterbury, and a part of said time resided in one of their families. That about the year 1801 my husband James Foster, united himself to said people by embracing their faith, but nevertheless continued with and provided for his family about six years after—that in the month of September, 1807, I consented to join their Society; and accordingly, with out four youngest children, we removed into their family. Not satisfied however with continuing there, I proposed after a residence of about three years among them, to withdraw from their society. To this they manifested some regret, but were nevertheless willing that I should depart, in case I could not unite in their belief. As I could not do this, I parted from them in peace, receiving at their hands such aid and assistance as satisfied me at the time, both as to their liberality and their justice. I further depose and say that during my residence among them I was treated with kindness, and had always the privilege of seeing my children when it was desired, although we resided in different families. And that since my leaving the said society I have at different times called upon them, for the purpose of seeing my children, three of whom still remain there, and was never opposed or denied; but on the contrary, kindly received and treated by the people, and saw and conversed with my children as long as I thought proper, except in one instance, when I was informed that my eldest daughter did not wish to see me. But I do not know that she was prohibited from so doing, had she desired it. I also add that I am satisfied that said society treat my children with care and tenderness, and feel a willingness, believing it will be for the best that they should remain there till the become of age, at which time they will be at liberty to choose for themselves.

I further depose and say, that I never supposed the marriage covenant to be impaired or annulled by embracing the principles and faith of the Shakers, nor did I ever understand, while a member of their community, or since, that such a sentiment was adopted by them.

BETSY FOSTER.

Rockingham, ss. June 21, 1817. Then Betsy Foster personally appearing, made solemn oath that the foregoing deposition by her subscribed, was just and true.—Before me,

S.A KIMBALL, Jus. Peace.

[No. 16]

I, *John Bishop*, of lawful age, testify and say, that I have lived in the society called Shakers, say 17 years with at New-York and Enfield, N.H. and am well acquainted with their faith and manner of life, which is clearly and truly stated in their publication entitled Christ's second appearing, (which I have read.) And I further say, that I am well acquainted with the Elders or ministry of the society at said Enfield; I do believe that they are sincere and honest, in what they profess, neither have I any reason to believe that they live in, teach or allow, any incestuous, wicked or sinful works in themselves, or those under their care.

JOHN BISHOP.

Grafton, ss. Lime, May 25th, 1818. Personally appeared John Bishop, and made solemn oath that the above affidavit by him subscribed is just and true.—Before

JONA. FRANKLIN, Jus. Peace

[No. 17]

I, *Abigail Bowden*, of lawful age, do testify, that when Moody Rich and Mary Dyer came to see her children I was present at the interview, and state that they both saw the children and freely conversed with them. At first Mary spoke to the children, saying, "this is your uncle Rich;" then he enquired of them concerning their welfare, their education, and likewise respecting their home, &c. Mary at the same time spoke to Betsey and told her if she was discontented, where she might find a home, mentioning her several uncles and also her grandmother.[43] Betsey answered her mother, saying that she had as good a home as she wanted—I also further state that at a certain time since the above occurred the said Mary came again to Enfield to see her children, and in my presence and hearing Mary spoke to Betsey concerning her home. Betsey replied, "I have told you a great many times that I was satisfied with my home," and said, "Do you not remember that I told you so when you and my uncle Moody were here?" The said Mary answered, "Yes, I remember it."

ABIGAIL BOWDEN.

[No. 18]

This may certify that I, *Nathaniel Draper*, was present and in hearing the greater part of the above statements, when Moody Rich and Mary Dyer came to Enfield to see her children; that it is an undeniable fact they both saw the children and conversed with them without any prohibition whatsoever—which was the only time the said Rich has been known to be at Enfield among our Society.

NATHANIAL DRAPER.
Enfield, Nov. 20, 1818.

State of New-Hampshire: Grafton, ss

Then personally appearing the above named Abigail Bowden and Nathaniel Draper, made solemn affirmation that the above statements by them subscribed are just and true. Before me,

DIARCA ALLEN, Justice Peace.

[No. 19]

I, *Caleb M. Dyer*, (son of Joseph and Mary Dyer) now in the nineteenth year of my age, do depose and say, that I am fully satisfied with the agreement of my parents in placing me under the care and providence of the society in which I now reside, and with the kind treatment which I ever have received from the people since I have been placed under their care. I am fully satisfied with my home; I want no other; neither have I seen the time one minute since I have lived with them that I wanted to go away. I am under no kind of bondage; but have full liberty to enjoy my faith according to the dictates of my own conscience. I further say, that I am fully acquainted with the treatment of my other brothers, and do say that we are better taken care of, both in sickness and health, than we could have been in our own father's house. I know of no abuse to children in the society; but they are well provided for with food and raiment; and generally have between nine and ten hours to sleep, for which there is no stated time for children, and are not required to work beyond their strength, of which I have full knowledge; my little brothers being a part of the time under my directions. I have often heard them say that they were pleased to live here; that they did not want to go away. And further, as it has been reported that my brother Orville was shut up in a closet in January, where he suffered much with the cold, when he was about six years old, I have conversed with him respecting the matter, and he says that he cannot remember any thing about it. Also, that he was in his ninth year when he came to live among the Shakers. And further, when any of my kindred came to see me and wished to know if I was satisfied and contented, I always answered them just as I felt in my own feelings impartially. My uncle Moody Rich came here with my mother to see us, and I and my sister and brothers conversed with them and told them that we were satisfied with our home.

CALEB M. DYER.[44]
Nov. 14, 1818.

State of New-Hampshire: Grafton, ss.
Nov. 14, 1818. Then the above named Caleb M. Dyer personally appeared and made solemn affirmation that the above declaration by him subscribed contains the truth and nothing but the truth. Before me,

E. EVANS, Not. Pub.

[No. 20]

I, *Betsey Dyer*, (daughter of Joseph and Mary Dyer) now in the seventeenth year of my age, depose and say, that I am greatly pleased with my home and feel thankful to my parents that they by their agreement have placed me under the care of such a kind people, where I am provided with every thing to make me happy, and I never have seen the time since I lived with them that I had the least feeling to leave them. I further say, that I never have seen any abuse offered by my father or by the society to my mother; but she was treated with the greatest kindness: and knowing the kindness that has been shewn to her and the children, it fills me with grief to find that she is trying to afflict my father and the society. I often say to myself, how can she do it! And further, as it is reported that we are kept in bondage among the Shakers, that we dare not speak as we feel, and that we dare not say any thing only what we are told to say, this is false; for I have always spoken to my kindred freely

without any embarrassment on the account of the Shakers. My uncle
Moody Rich came here with my mother to see us; we conversed with
them freely as much as we pleased. My mother told me where I might go
if I was discontented to live here. I told her that I was fully satisfied with
my home. In the close of our conversation, my uncle asked me what
word I had to send my friends. I told him that he might tell them I was
well and had a good home, and did not want any better. And further,
since the above time my mother came to see us, and she speaking concerning my home, I asked her if she did not remember that I told her
when she came to see us with my uncle Moody Rich, that I was satisfied
with my home? She replied, "Yes, I remember it."

BETSEY DYER.[45]
Nov. 14, 1818.

State of New-Hampshire: Grafton, ss.
Nov. 14, 1818. Then personally appeared the above named Betsey Dyer
and made solemn affirmation that the above declaration by her subscribed contains the truth and nothing but the truth. Before me,

E. EVANS, Not. Public.

[No. 21]

I, *Betsey Tillotson*, of lawful age, do testify and say, that some time in the
spring of the year, A.D. 1817, Mary Dyer was at our house, and in conversation relative to her controversy with the Shakers (so called) that
she said she was determined to break up their society, but if she should
be disappointed, and could not carry her point against them, she would
SET FIRE TO THEM.

BETSEY TILLOTSON

Coos ss. May 28, 1818. Then personally appeared the above named
Betsey Tillotson and made solemn oath, that the foregoing affidavit by
her subscribed is true, before me,

WM. LOVEJOY, Jus. Peace.

A REMONSTRANCE *against the testimony and application of* MARY DYER, *requesting Legislative interference against the united society called* SHAKERS.[46]

To the Honorable, the Legislature of New-Hampshire,
now in session.

Whereas, it is evident that Mary Dyer has undertaken to defame the character of the united Society commonly called Shakers, and through the aid of some malicious persons who have separated themselves from the said Society, by reason of their own base and immoral conduct, has furnished herself with false testimonies, and other vague and defamatory insinuations, calculated to inflame the minds of the ignorant and uninformed; and whereas the said Mary prayed for relief, under a specious pretext of grievances, in a petition to the Legislature, June session 1817, which contained well known false statements, accompanied with other documents, apparently designed for the purpose of getting a law passed to deprive the said society of their equal protection of government; and as she still continues to solicit legislative aid by a similar complaint;—

Therefore, we the undersigned, members of the said united society called Shakers, having certain knowledge of those things wherein the society are misrepresented, feel it our duty, as the friends of justice and truth, to remonstrate against the aforesaid false testimonies, and all documents contributing to the support, as a public slander on the society in general, and an open attack upon our lawful rights and privileges in particular.

We do not make a practice of intruding upon the public with any of the peculiarities of our institution, or even refuting the vague and inconsistent reports that are propagated upon us: but when our *religious creed,* (so called) *exercises, and conduct in general,* are taken under examination by men in office, and publicly proscribed under specious charges of moral evil; and when legislative interference is invoked to decree our punishment for crimes of which *we are not guilty,* we feel bound to contradict their deceptious statements, and to represent those things in their true colors, for which we are called in question; as we believe that the time is

come for civil rulers to know our principles and conduct to the foundation, and be no longer imposed upon by those false accusations which
have stained the earth with the blood of millions of harmless beings.

The crimes, virtually alleged against us, by Mary Dyer and others of
a similar disposition are truly great; such as blasphemy, perjury, fornication, adultery or double marriage, cruelty and abuse: in fact, we are in-
directly charged with all manner of evil, inasmuch as we are charged
with holding principles, from which every evil must necessarily flow:
but, if those evils do flow from our principles, why do not our adversaries
detect and punish us according to the laws that be? They may pretend
that certain facts are substantiated by sufficient testimony, but we object
to their testimony as illegal and unworthy of credit: nor can they prove
one fact by a legal process. Mary Dyer and her associates, have abundantly manifested, both by threats and actions, that they have been under the influence of malice; neither have the charges brought against us
by the said Mary, as yet been subject to a full investigation; but some
things have been mutilated and colored in a high degree, and many others are notoriously false, and without foundation; consequently we feel
clear of her false imputations, and challenge her or any other person to
substantiate the abominable principles and conduct which she has slan-
derously palmed upon us.

The insinuations of fornication, adultery, double marriage, and such
irregularities, used by Mary Dyer, to cloak her insolent conduct towards
us are groundless; and if the order of any family is changed in any respect, in consequence of becoming members of our society, it is by the
free consent or choice of the parties, and for the purpose of forming an
order which we believe is calculated to bring us nearer to God, and not
for the purpose of any unlawful indulgence.

But we are impelled, by the demands of truth and justice (as well to
the public, as to ourselves) to state, that the aforesaid Mary Dyer is the
only person in our knowledge, who pretended to hold any relation to
this Society, that ever attempted to propagate, and establish the pernicious principle of bigamy, or irregular connexions under the cloak of
spiritual marriage; this she strove hard to maintain in direct opposition
to every principle and precept of both law and gospel, and also diametri-
cally contrary to anything ever admitted by the society, till at length her
loss of confidence and lack of union induced her to leave the said soci-

ety; declaring at the same time that she did know what excuse to make to others for her leaving the people; "for (said she) I have never seen any thing evil among you; but as you have always treated me with kindness, I will treat you in like manner," &c.

But being left without a reasonable excuse and failing in her apparent design of drawing her husband and family after her, she soon undertook to shift her quarters, and try to throw back her foul character upon us.

Therefore, to insinuate that we are guilty of such abominations, and then commit the horrid act of perjury for the concealment of our crimes, is malicious in the extreme!

Had Mary Dyer realized the horrors of perjury, she never would have stated under oath that the Shaker elders charged her not to expose the freedom which they had attempted to make with her, that if she did, they would make her the liar; nor yet that any person under the title of father or mother among the Shakers ever said that they were Christ: or that they selected out a man for her; nor with any more truth could she have stated that the elders or any other members of our society believe it pleasing to God to tell a lie to screen them from apparent evils! Nor yet that children were compelled to rise at half past four in the winter, and half past three in the summer.

Moreover, if she had meant to support the character of a woman in veracity, she would not have said that she was compelled to follow her children who were previously taken to the Society of Shakers in New-Enfield; for it is a notorious fact, that she in person, brought three of them there herself; and her own hand writing now in our possession may prove that she was previously anxious to convey the other two, even beyond our freedom at that time; all of which false statements may be seen in a deposition over her signature included in a pamphlet now before the public, said to be written by Eunice Chapman, comprising libellous slanders of a like nature.

In fact the said Mary Dyer or any other person could never have stated under oath nor otherwise, one sentence contained in the aforesaid deposition respecting us without the wilful perversion of truth, as may appear evident from her own testimony, and also from the very nature of our institution.

Our real principles and practice we never deny; but the false colors in which our accusers have represented us, we do deny. We believe the Holy Scriptures to be a record of divine truth; and we appeal to no other *religious creed* for the propriety, either of our faith or practice; yet we are charged with the greatest infidelity, and even atheism, from our respect to the visible head of the society, as though we believed in no Supreme Being superior to man.

We believe in one true God, who is a Spirit, the fountain of all good,—and we believe also in Jesus Christ as the only Saviour of mankind. Moreover, we believe that the only true God was in Christ, and that the only true Christ (who is a Spirit) was in the apostles,—and wherever that Spirit is manifested, either in man or woman, we acknowledge *that* as the true head,—and we think it safe to follow the teaching of *that Spirit,* as Jesus said to his disciples, *It is not ye that speak, but the spirit of your Father, which speaketh in you,*—therefore, St. Paul said, *Be ye followers of me even as I am of Christ.*

Now if our adversaries would candidly compare our principles with the Scriptures, they could not think that we are so deluded as they represent us to be. We teach no other doctrine than what Jesus Christ and his apostles taught, nor obey any other than what is comprised in their words,—therefore, we obey them that are over us in the Lord, doing service as unto God, and not to men.

And admitting that millions under despotic governments, have been deluded by false apostles, and deceitful workers—that is no certain evidence that we are: as the subjects of a free government, we claim the indisputable right of doing what we believe in our conscience to by our duty; and to refrain from every thing which we deem sinful or offensive to God: and according to this rule we offer the following candid and true statement of our principles and conduct concerning the marriage covenant, and the treatment of children, with a few remarks on our treatment toward the said Mary Dyer subsequent to her leaving our society.

1st. With regard to the marriage covenant, our faith on this subject is precisely the same with that of St. Paul to the Corinthians, chap. 7th, where he says, if a brother hath a wife that believeth not, and she be pleased to dwell with him, let him not put her away: and the woman which hath an husband that believeth not, and if he be pleased to dwell with her, let her not leave him; but if the unbelieving depart, let them depart.

This is our faith and an established principle with us; and whoever joins our society being bound by the law, we consider them bound to fulfil all that the law requires of them relative to the marriage covenant: and as the law does not require sexual cohabitation contrary to the dictates of conscience; therefore, there is nothing required in the law respecting the marriage contract, that is contrary to our faith, nor in our faith repugnant to the law;—Wherefore, we do not pretend to dissolve or disannul any thing that either the law or gospel requires in this respect, notwithstanding the statement of Mary Dyer and others to the contrary: but on the other hand we counsel those who come in among us, to fulfil all that the law requires of them, as well in regard to the marriage contract as anything else: the truth of this is self-evident; for after the said Mary had eloped, and had been lawfully advertised by her husband Joseph Dyer, for his own safety; and had tendered herself upon his advertisement, claiming his lawful protection, and promising obedience, he considered himself responsible, and made provision for her maintenance for about two years; and still would have continued to provide for her, had had she not utterly refused his provision, or to comply with any of his lawful demands. And notwithstanding her non-compliance with every just measure of her husband's providing for her; yet he has to our knowledge, frequently proposed to make a just and equitable settlement of property with her; the decision of which, he has offered to submit to the judgment of impartial men: but this she has also refused.

2nd. The treatment of children we consider a point of great importance, and our right to govern our children, until they are of lawful age, we hold sacred.

The duty of children to their parents, no just law can ever disannul, and the obligation is by no means lessened by the gospel nor yet by our institution; therefore the duty of obedience from children to their parents, we teach and enforce in a manner, which our consciences will approve, on the strictest examination, before any men of truth or candor.

We know of no child held in our society, but what has been given up by the request or free consent of its parents; nor do we know of any who are held contrary to their own free choice: nor yet, to our knowledge, has any among us, in a single instance, ever been secluded from seeing their parents, or relations from without the society whenever requested in a civil manner.

Furthermore we consider ourselves entire strangers to any thing on our part, or through our means, that could be called imprisonment or abuse, by any person of candor, offered either to Mary Dyer or any other person.

The said Mary's being fastened up in her room, at a certain time with a man who was not of our Society, and who was unwilling to tell, either his business or his name, was not our fault; for the fastenings were ever on her own side of the door; but she always had free access to the door-yard and highway, and went wherever she pleased while on our premises.

And notwithstanding her complaint of being put under a mistress, and having a stint set her, the only work she did of her husband's providing, (except to wash her own clothes) was to spin twenty run for the term of about two months: during this time she was provided with a horse to go to Hanover, besides going once or twice in the stage; she also frequently visited different parts of the town of Enfield in the above mentioned time.

This she is pleased to call imprisonment.

It may also be observed, that the property of the said Joseph and Mary Dyer, lies principally in wild lands in Stewartstown; that the said Joseph holds his own deeds, and that we never had any thing to do with it.

To enter into all the particular charges, and false insinuations, exhibited by Mary Dyer and others, we think unnecessary; and as we seek no revenge, and for the honor of her sex, we forbear to particularize her unseemly conduct previous to her leaving the said Society: but those few principal things, which may serve as a key to all the rest, we have stated for the information of the Legislature, that nothing might be done, which would leave any ground of reflection on us, for our silence or neglect of duty.

Therefore, as the subjects of a just moral government, we individually hold ourselves accountable for our moral conduct: and as we pretend to no new invention in church matters, but have our example from the primitive apostolic church, and as we have violated no existing law, we have no apprehension that the wise Legislature of this State, will give themselves the unnecessary trouble of projecting a list of new crimes and punishments on our account. But should it be thought proper for the satisfaction of all concerned, to appoint a court or committee of examination, to search into any secret causes of complaint, that may be thought to exist among us, there is nothing pertaining either to our institution or conduct, but shall be laid open, and free to inspection at any time: we shall deem it a privilege, to manifest our freedom that all who are of age, and even children whose parents are not among us, (unless enticed by unlawful means,) are at full liberty to stay, or go, according to their own faith and free choice: and consequently, that any compulsory law either way, would be an abridgement of our inherent rights.

Therefore, confiding in that wisdom, candor, and patriotic zeal, with which Almighty God hath inspired the rulers of this great nation, and with expressions of our grateful thanks for the blessings which we have long enjoyed, under just and equal administrations, we subscribe ourselves the obedient subjects of the constituted authorities of the United States, and of this State, and the friends of Justice, peace and truth.

In behalf of the said United Society. June 17, 1818.

Nathaniel Draper, Trueworthy Heath, John Lyon, Moses Jewett, Jason Kidder, John Barker, Overseers of said Society in Enfield.

Francis Winkley, Israel Sanborn, John Whitcher, Ezra Wiggin, Thomas Kidder, William Fletcher, Overseers of said Society in Canterbury.

POETRY.[47]

1. WE read of a people in ages long past,
   Who wished their neighbors no ill,
   Yet were persecuted and daily harrass'd,
   And driven from mountain to hill:
   These innocent souls had no lawful defence;
   But if persecutors now say,
   Abandon your faith, or we'll banish you hence—
   In reason we answer them, Nay.
2. The Lord was not deaf to his people's complaints,
   When in former ages oppress'd;
   But graciously promis'd his innocent saints

A day of salvation and rest.
When this blessed season has truly begun,
And God puts an end to the fray,
Must peaceable men to the wilderness run?
Each promise of God answers, Nay.

3. We have not the laws of a Nero to face,
Nor the horrid edicts of Rome;
This new dispensation has alter'd the case,
And fix'd us a peaceable home.
While men of sound reason are widely awake,
Asserting the rights of the day,
Must harmless believers their country forsake?
The good Constitution says, Nay.

4. The righteous for their indispensable right,
May lawfully enter their plea;
Yet they are not bound for their freedom to fight,
Nor are they obliged to flee:
The laws of the country the wicked must meet,
And shall their strong pillars give way?
Must all civil rulers before them retreat?
The voice of the Nation is Nay.

5. The law and the gospel do now harmonize,
And each has its work to perform;
To root out the gospel if wicked men rise,
The law has to scatter the storm:
The gospel does honor the laws of the land,
The law does the gospel survey;
Then ask if this gospel may lawfully stand,
The law has to answer us, Yea.

6. If all the transactions in heaven and earth,
For almost these two thousand years,
Have been to give virtuous liberty birth,
How solid her standing appears!
Then come, ye afflicted and scatter'd abroad,
You ask, if in peace you may stay;
From all the extensive dominions of God,
The answer is pointedly, Yea.

7. Though sinners may roar like the waves of the sea,
  And spread the most dreadful alarm;
  Touch not mine anointed, is heaven's decree;
  And do my good prophets no harm.
  Then let them abuse the true saints of the Lord,
  As it must be granted they may;
  But shall they not have the transgressors' reward?
  The people must all answer, Yea.
8. "Away with this fellow! his doctrine I hate!"
  Through despotic kingdoms would roar;
  But under the laws of this free happy state,
  The cry is defended no more:
  The true independence of this happy land,
  The nation is bound to defend;
  In this independence we'll virtuously stand,
  And heaven and earth say, AMEN!

NOTES

PREFACE

1. The text of the Concord edition was reset for the Boston edition. The pagination of the two editions is the same, with only occasional minor differences in the last word in a line of text. There are slight differences in punctuation and capitalization, and typesetting errors vary between the two editions. The Concord edition uses ʃ to represent the letter s when it appears within a word; the Boston edition uses only s. There were at least two printings of the Boston edition with two variant title pages marked by differences in font size and italicization. To compare the Concord and Boston editions, see both at the American Antiquarian Society (Worcester, Mass.). To compare the two Boston editions, compare the copy in the collection of the American Antiquarian Society with that held in the Burke Library of Hamilton College (Clinton, N.Y.).
2. The 1818 and 1819 editions of *A Compendious Narrative* are identical and likely indicate that the printer reset the date to account for the unexpected delay in publication. The text in this volume was transcribed from a copy with the 1818 title page date. On the publication delay, see a letter from the Ministry at Canterbury, N.H., to the Ministry at New Lebanon, N.Y., February 19, 1819, microfilm reel IV:A-3, Shaker Manuscripts, Western Reserve Historical Society, Cleveland, Ohio.

INTRODUCTION

1. Mary Marshall Dyer to Mills Olcott, August 1819, MS. 819490.1, Dartmouth College Library, Hanover, N.H.
2. On the early years of Shakerism see Stephen Stein, *The Shaker Experience in America* (New Haven: Yale University Press, 1992); population statistics are found in Priscilla J. Brewer, *Shaker Communities, Shaker Lives* (Hanover, N.H.: University Press of New England, 1986), 215. For detailed treatments of the religious context of Shakerism, see Clarke Garrett, *Spirit Possession and Popular Religion: From the Camisards to the Shakers* (Balti-

more: Johns Hopkins University Press, 1987), and Stephen Marini, *Radical Sects in Revolutionary New England* (Cambridge: Harvard University Press, 1982).

3. *Dartmouth Gazette and Grafton and Coos Advertiser*, February 18, 1815. An original of the newspaper with this notice survives in the archives of the State of New Hampshire, Division of Records Management and Archives, Concord, N.H.

4. Ibid., March 21, 1815.

5. Hanover, New Hampshire, is eight miles west of the Enfield Shaker community and home to Dartmouth College (founded 1769).

6. Joseph Dyer, *A Compendious Narrative*, 85. All page references to *A Compendious Narrative* refer to the text reprinted in the present edition. For details about the original edition, see my preface, together with note 2.

7. For the official record of her petition for assistance, see *Journal of the House of Representatives of the State of New Hampshire. June 1817* (Concord, N.H.: Isaac Hill, 1817); and *Journal of the Senate of the State of New Hampshire. June 1817* (Concord, N.H.: Isaac Hill, 1817).

8. "The Shakers," *New Hampshire Patriot*, July 1, 1817.

9. On the challenges of marriage in this period see Mary Beth Sievens, *Stray Wives: Marital Conflict in Early National New England* (New York: New York University Press, 2005). On New Hampshire divorce law see *First Constitutional Period, 1784–1792*, vol. 5 of *Laws of New Hampshire* (Concord, N.H.: Evans Printing Co., 1921), 732–33 (An Act to Prevent Incestuous Marriages and to Regulate Divorces); *Second Constitutional Period, 1821–1828*, vol. 9 of *Laws of New Hampshire*, 357 (An Act in Addition to An Act, Entitled An Act to Prevent Incestuous Marriages); and State of New Hampshire, Revised Statutes Online, Section 458:7, Absolute Divorce, Generally, www.gencourt.state.nh.us/rsa/html/XLiii/458/458-7.htm. For a history of marriage and divorce see Norma Basch, *Framing American Divorce: From the Revolutionary Generation to the Victorians* (Berkeley: University of California Press, 1999); Nancy Cott, *Public Vows: A History of Marriage and the Nation* (Cambridge: Harvard University Press, 2002); Hendrik Hartog, *Man and Wife in America: A History* (Cambridge: Harvard University Press, 2002); Roderick Phillips, *Putting Asunder: A History of Divorce in Western Society* (New York: Cambridge University Press, 1988); and idem, *Untying the Knot: A Short History of Divorce* (New York: Cambridge University Press, 1991).

10. On *Willis v. Dyer*, see Elizabeth A. De Wolfe, *Shaking the Faith: Women, Family and Mary Marshall Dyer's Anti-Shaker Campaign, 1815–1867* (New York: Palgrave, 2002), 99–103.

11. Eunice Hawley Chapman, *An Account of the People Called Shakers* (Albany, N.Y.: Printed for the Authoress, at 95 State Street, 1817). The following year Chapman published *No. 2: Being the Additional Account of the Conduct of the Shakers* (Albany, N.Y.: Printed by I. W. Clark for the Authoress, 1818).

12. In Abram Van Vleet, *Account of the Conduct of the Shakers* (Lebanon, Ohio: Abram Van Vleet, 1818), 13. Van Vleet's book is discussed at greater length later in this introduction.

13. Ibid., 14.

14. Ibid., 25.

15. *The Memorial of James Chapman, to the Respectable Legislature of the State of New York, Now in Session* ([Albany, N.Y.]: n.p., 1817), 1.

16. Ibid., 2.

17. Ibid.

18. Ibid.

19. Ibid.

20. On this event see Elizabeth A. De Wolfe, "The Mob at Enfield: Community, Gender, and Violence against the Shakers," in *Intentional Community: An Anthropological Perspective*, ed. Susan Love Brown (Albany: State University of New York Press, 2002), 107–30. See also Jean M. Humez, "'A Woman Mighty to Pull You Down': Married Women's Rights and Female Anger in the Anti-Shaker Narratives of Eunice Chapman and Mary Marshall Dyer," *Journal of Women's History* 6, no. 2 (Summer 1994): 90–110.

21. For the petition see Mary Dyer, *A Brief Statement*, 58–59. (All page references to *A Brief Statement* refer to the text reprinted in the present edition. For details about the original edition, see my preface, together with note 1.) The legislature dismissed this petition; see the discussion in De Wolfe, *Shaking the Faith*, 97–99.

22. For the legislative record of her appearance, see *Journal of the Senate of the State of New Hampshire, June Session, 1818* (Concord, N.H.: Isaac Hill, 1818), 222–32.

23. Norma Basch notes that divorce-trial pamphlets were offered for sale inexpensively and, like the Dyers' texts, were intended for an eagerly buying audience. See Basch, *Framing American Divorce*, 147.

24. The Shakers' rebuttal was also printed in the local newspaper: "A Remonstrance," *New Hampshire Patriot*, June 30, 1818.

25. Joseph Dyer, *A Compendious Narrative*, 65–66.

26. Ann Fabian, *The Unvarnished Truth: Personal Narratives in Nineteenth-Century America* (Berkeley: University of California Press, 2000).

27. Valentine Rathbun, *An Account of the Matter, Form, and Manner of a New*

and Strange Religion (Providence, R.I.: Printed and Sold by Bennet Wheeler, 1781).

28. Amos Taylor, *A Narrative of the Strange Principles, Conduct, and Character of the People Known by the Name of Shakers* (Worcester, Mass.: Printed for the Author [by Isaiah Thomas], 1782); Benjamin West, *Scriptural Cautions against Embracing a Religious Scheme* (Hartford, Conn.: Printed and Sold by Bavil Webster, 1783); Daniel Rathbun, *A Letter from Daniel Rathbun* (Springfield, Mass.: Printed at the Printing-Office Near the Great Ferry, 1785); Reuben Rathbun, *Reasons Offered for Leaving the Shakers* (Pittsfield, Mass.: Printed by Chester Smith, 1800). The anti-Shaker writings of James Smith include *Remarkable Occurrences Lately Discovered among the People Called Shakers . . .* (Carthage, Tenn.: Printed by William Moore, 1810), and *Shakerism Detected, Their Erroneous and Treasonous Proceedings, and False Publications* (Paris, Ky.: Printed by Joel R. Lyle, 1810).

29. Benjamin Seth Youngs, *Testimony of Christ's Second Appearing: Containing a General Statement of All Things Pertaining to the Faith and Practice of the Church of God in this Latter-Day* (Lebanon, Ohio: From the Press of John M'Clean, 1808). Following Shaker practice, Youngs's name did not appear on the title page.

30. Examples include Christopher Clark, *A Shock to Shakerism; or, A Serious Refutation of the Idolatrous Divinity of Ann Lee of Manchester* (Richmond, Ky.: Printed for T. W. Ruble, 1812); and Samuel Brown, *A Countercheck to Shakerism* (Cincinnati: Looker and Reynolds, 1824).

31. Thomas Brown, *An Account of the People Called Shakers* (Troy, N.Y.: Parker and Bliss, 1810).

32. Letter from the Ministry New Lebanon to Ministry Union Village, March 27, 1819, microfilm reel IV:A-33, Shaker Manuscripts, Western Reserve Historical Society, Cleveland, Ohio.

33. Shaker works available to the public included the 1808 edition of Benjamin Seth Youngs's lengthy treatise *Testimony of Christ's Second Appearing,* a "corrected and improved" second edition of this work published in Albany, N.Y., in 1810, and the third edition printed at Union Village, Ohio, in 1823. A shorter, more accessible introduction to Shakerism was provided by Calvin Green and Seth Y. Wells, *A Summary View of the Millennial Church, or United Society of Believers (Commonly Called Shakers)* (Albany, N.Y.: Printed by Packard & Van Benthuysen, 1823). For an extensive two-volume bibliography of printed works by and about the Shakers see Mary Richmond, *Shaker Literature* (Hancock, Mass.: Shaker Community, Inc., 1977). On visitors' accounts of the Shakers see Glendyne R. Wergland, ed., *Visiting the Shakers, 1778–1849* (Hamilton, N.Y.: Richard W. Couper Press, 2007).

34. This is an important distinction between the two women. In the Chapmans' case, James had indeed taken their children without Eunice's knowledge. While she followed his trail to the Watervliet Shaker village and
may have spent a few days at the Shaker community, she did not join the
faith. Her argument for divorce was based on abandonment and kidnap-
ping, and she was successful; in 1817, the New York legislature granted
Eunice a divorce and custody of her children. Mary Dyer, on the other
hand, had joined the Shakers at Enfield and lived among them for two
years. In her publications, she is careful to frame her story as a victim of
her husband's cruel will: that Joseph was going to take the children to the
Shaker village with her or without her. Mary claimed she went only to
protect her children as best she could. To show her husband's poor parent-
ing skills, she maintained that Joseph, who had "no will of his own," suc-
cumbed to the temptation of alcohol, and subsequently to the mesmeric
power of the Shaker elders who had deluded him. Mary, of course, claimed
right from the start that she had "impressions" of the Shaker's true nature.
Mary Dyer, A Brief Statement, 31.

35. Joseph Dyer, A Compendious Narrative, 91.

36. Ibid., 67.

37. The anonymous manuscript message is written on a copy of the Remonstrance against the Testimony and Application of Mary Dyer (Boston: Printed
for N. Coverely, 1818) in the collection of the American Antiquarian Society, Worcester, Mass. Daniel Robinson's annotated copy of the Remonstrance is in the Communal Societies Collection, Burke Library, Hamilton
College, Clinton, N.Y.

38. See, for example, the correspondence between Concord, New Hampshire,
resident Mary Clark and her Boston friends, Francis and Eliza Jackson.
Clark shared her positive opinions of Mary Dyer and sent copies of Dyer's
publications to the Jacksons. The Papers of Francis Jackson, manuscripts
in the collection of the Massachusetts Historical Society, Boston.

39. Mancer, Joseph's son from his first marriage, is never mentioned. By 1818
he was past the age of majority and able to leave or stay at the Shaker village as he desired. He remained with the Enfield Shakers until the late
1820s, and then he disappears from the historical record.

40. Basch, Framing American Divorce, 62.

41. See Absolem Blackburn, A Brief Account of the . . . People Usually Denomi-
nated Shakers (Flemingsburg, Ky.: Printed by A. Crookshanks, 1824).

42. Indoctrum Parliamentum: A Farce, In One Act and a Beautiful Variety of
Scenes [Albany, N.Y.: 1818].

43. "The Shakers," New Hampshire Patriot, July 1, 1817.

44. "A Statement Concerning the Mob at Enfield" (1818), manuscript, Communal Societies Collection, Burke Library, Hamilton College.
45. Folsom's advertisement was published May 6, 1828, and recorded by the Shaker historian Henry Blinn in "Historical Notes on Believers Having Reference to Believers at Enfield," vol. 1, p. 196, typescript (photocopy), Shaker library, United Society of Shakers, Sabbathday Lake, Maine. On the 1828 petitions to the legislature, see De Wolfe, *Shaking the Faith*, 128–29.
46. Richard McNemar, *The Other Side of the Question* (Cincinnati, Ohio: Looker, Reynolds, and Co., 1819), 3. McNemar's book also contains a reprint of Joseph Dyer's *A Compendious Narrative*, although without the 1818 *Remonstrance to the New Hampshire Legislature* included at the end of Dyer's original text.
47. Mary M. Dyer, *A Portraiture of Shakerism, Exhibiting a General View of Their Character and Conduct, from the First Appearance of Ann Lee in New-England, down to Present Time* ([Haverhill, N.H.]: Printed for the Author [by Sylvester T. Goss], 1822). The full title of the Shakers' rebuttal is *A Review of Mary Dyer's Publication, entitled "A Portraiture of Shakerism"; together with Sundry Affidavits, Disproving the Truth of Her Assertions* (Concord, N.H.: Printed by J. B. Moore for the Society, 1824); Mary's response to it is titled *Reply to the Shakers' Statements, Called a "Review of the Portraiture of Shakerism," with an Account of the Sickness and Death of Betsy Dyer . . .* (Concord, N.H.: Printed for the Author, 1824).
48. Susan Bramley (Alfred, Maine) to Sophia Frost (York, Maine), ca. 1824, manuscript letter, private collection.
49. On the 1820s print battle between Mary Dyer and the Shakers, see Elizabeth A. De Wolfe, "Mary Marshall Dyer, Gender, and *A Portraiture of Shakerism*," *Religion and American Culture* 8, no. 2 (Summer 1998): 237–64. Mary's publications in the 1820s also include two broadsides, "To the Elders and Principals of the Shaker Societies" (copy in the collections of the Houghton Library, Harvard University) and "To the Public" (copy in the collections of the American Antiquarian Society, Worcester, Mass.), both printed in New Lebanon, N.Y., in 1826. In addition to *A Review of Mary Dyer's Publication, entitled "A Portraiture of Shakerism,"* Shaker responses included a broadside by James Farnham, "To the Public. Having lately Seen a Scandalous Handbill in Circulation, Published by Mary Dyer, Containing, Among Other Malicious Falsehoods, A Slanderous Charge against Me" (n.p., 1825; copy in the Shaker Collection of the Western Reserve Historical Society, Cleveland, Ohio).
50. Mary Marshall, *The Rise and Progress of the Serpent from the Garden of Eden, to Present Day* (Concord, N.H.: Printed for the Author, 1847). To

remind potential readers of her former notoriety, Mary included on the title page of this book a statement clarifying the name of "the author, who was Mary M. Dyer but now is Mary Marshall."

51. Mary Dyer, *Shakerism Exposed* (Hanover, N.H.: Dartmouth Press, ca. 1852). Perhaps reflecting fading interest in and memory of her long anti-Shaker campaign, Mary published her final work under the name of Mary Dyer, the name to which she had legally changed in 1852. For a detailed biography of Mary Dyer's life and an account of her anti-Shaker campaign, see De Wolfe, *Shaking the Faith*.

52. Dyer, *Brief Statement*, 39.

53. "Found Dead," *Granite State Free Press*, January 18, 1867.

MARY M. DYER, *A Brief Statement*

1. This text was distributed to members of the New Hampshire Legislature prior to Mary Dyer's June 1818 hearing (see the introduction).

2. The preacher is Lemuel Crooker, who returned to New Hampshire with copies of *The Testimony of Christ's Second Appearing*, likely the second edition published in 1810 in New York State. In the nineteenth century, non-Shakers referred to this lengthy theological treatise as the Shaker Bible. See Stephen Stein, "Inspiration, Revelation, and Scripture: The Story of a Shaker Bible," *Proceedings of the American Antiquarian Society* 105, part 2 (1996): 347–76.

3. *I have since heard him say he treated me so at that time, he thought I should come to some untimely end.* [Dyer's note.]

4. Elders and eldresses were community leaders in Shaker villages. Shaker communities were divided into self-sufficient "families," each with its own leadership, industries, and living quarters, and each of these families was led by two elders and two eldresses.

5. There is no surviving record of Joseph Dyer's visit to the Alfred Shaker community, located in southwestern Maine, which was founded in 1793 and had a population of 129 members in 1810. At the time of Joseph's visit there were three Shaker communities in Maine: Alfred, Gorham, and Sabbathday Lake. Gorham (founded in 1808) was the first Shaker community to close, in 1819. The Alfred community closed in 1931, and its remaining members joined the community at Sabbathday Lake, in the town of New Gloucester, which has remained active since its founding in 1794 and in the twenty-first century is the only remaining active Shaker community.

6. The War of 1812, fought between 1812 and 1815.

7. The word "friends" refers to family members. Joseph Dyer was born June

19, 1772, in Canterbury, Connecticut. He was the youngest of eight children of Captain Elijah Dyer (1716–1793) and Elizabeth Williams (1733–1817). Joseph used money inherited from his father to settle in northern New Hampshire in 1796.

8. The older brother is Caleb Marshall Dyer (1800–1863).

9. The children of Mary and Joseph Dyer: Caleb Marshall Dyer, Betsey Dyer (1802–1824), Orville Dyer (1804–1882), Jerrub Dyer (1806–1886), and Joseph Dyer Jr. (1809–1840).

10. *This family were believers of the Shaker's faith in Stewartstown, Coos.* [Dyer's note.] Daniel Taylor was a Stewartstown, New Hampshire, neighbor and Joseph's hired hand. Taylor and his family joined the Enfield Shakers along with the Dyers, part of a group of nearly thirty converts from northern New Hampshire.

11. In 1810, the Enfield Shaker community had 134 members divided among three families. Mary Dyer lived in the North, or novitiate, Family, where new members learned Shaker practices and beliefs. On the history of the Enfield Shakers see Wendell Hess, *The Enfield (N.H.) Shakers: A Brief History* (Enfield, N.H.: n.p., 1993).

12. In 1813, Caleb and Betsey Dyer were living with the village's South Family, Jerrub and Orville Dyer were housed in the Church family, and Mary, Joseph, and Joseph Jr. lived in the North Family.

13. Lucy Lyon, eldress of the community's North Family.

14. "The world's people" are all those outside of Shakerism.

15. Dyer is referring to the *Testimony of Christ's Second Appearing.*

16. The ministry leaders were referred to as Mother and Father, and in Shaker communities they lived in rooms above the meetinghouse. Ministry leaders handled spiritual matters in each community.

17. Romans 1:20–32 faults those who cannot clearly see the glory of God. Failing to acknowledge and honor the true God, these sinners turn to lust, wickedness, and evil, and encourage others to follow suit. Mary Dyer cites this passage to accuse the Shakers of what she terms "unnatural" practices, including secret homosexual relationships. In her attacks, Mary repeatedly accuses the Shaker leadership of publicly professing celibacy but secretly engaging in rituals to initiate new members into some sort of hidden, and unspecified, sexual practice. The Shakers responded to Mary's allegations by way of Joseph's *Compendious Narrative*, in which he accuses Mary of marital infidelity and of making a homosexual advance to a young Shaker woman. For early nineteenth-century readers, any deviation from the mainstream norm of married, heterosexual sexual relationships—celibacy, profligacy, homosexuality—was cause for fear and condemnation.

18. Mary's babe is her youngest child, Joseph Jr.

19. On this 1815 advertisement see the introduction.

20. Tow is the fiber of the flax plant, which is spun into thread and then woven to produce linen cloth.

21. On James Chapman and his wife, Eunice, see the introduction.

22. Mary's Monday visitor was likely Asa Tenney, a Quaker whom Mary had met in Hanover. Her Wednesday visitors were likely John Williams and Calvin Eaton, also new supporters from Hanover. See De Wolfe, *Shaking the Faith*, 44.

23. Joseph has arranged to board Mary with her sister Betsy and brother-in-law Obadiah Tillotson in Orford, New Hampshire, for one dollar per week.

24. Judge Edward Evans of Enfield. Evans often accompanied Mary Dyer on her visits to the Shakers. During the 1818 mob at Enfield, Evans represented the Shakers' interests. He did not appear to choose a side in this debate; rather he seems to have been primarily interested in maintaining the peace of society, and he worked to mediate the escalating battle between Mary and the Enfield Shakers.

25. Moses Jewett, one of the Shaker trustees, or business leaders of the community. Trustees were concerned with temporal matters, including purchases from and sales to communities beyond the Shaker village.

26. See Luke 2:25–35; the elderly Simeon met Jesus, Mary, and Joseph as they entered the Temple on the fortieth day after Jesus' birth, as had been foretold by the Holy Spirit, who had promised Simeon he would not die until meeting the Savior. Simeon held the baby Jesus and offered a blessing that foreshadowed the crucifixion.

27. John 19:26–27.

28. Jesus raised Lazarus from the dead (see John 11:1–44).

29. Joseph Peverly is Joseph Dyer's former father-in-law, the father of his first wife, Elizabeth.

30. Betsy Tillotson is Mary Dyer's sister.

31. Christopher Baily is Mary Dyer's brother-in-law.

32. Moody Rich is Mary Dyer's brother-in-law, the husband of her sister Sally.

33. As this dialogue shows, Mary Dyer took an active role in the collection of depositions, posing questions to solicit the information she needed to make her case.

34. The lack of compensation for communal labor performed was a frequent complaint lodged against the Shakers by former members.

35. Pattee is relaying a widespread story that the original Shakers engaged in naked dancing.

36. Many anti-Shaker authors reported stories that Ann Lee drank to excess. See, for example, Daniel Rathbun, *A Letter from Daniel Rathbun* (Springfield, Mass.: Printed at the Printing-Office Near the Great Ferry, 1785).

37. Extracts from the *Testimony of Christ's Second Appearing*. As Mary Dyer picks apart the Shakers' text, we see the double-edged sword of publishing: the *Testimony* proselytizes and can bring the Shakers new converts, but it also provides grist for the mills of opposition and can draw readers away from Shakerism.

38. Mary refers to her 1817 appearance before the New Hampshire Legislature (see the introduction).

39. The legislature, moved by Dyer's impassioned plea for assistance, passed a bill proposing an amendment to New Hampshire's divorce law. Governor William Plumer, who allowed this bill to expire without his signature (see the introduction), argued that passing such a law required investigation, not simply reacting to the emotional response one particular case stimulated. On Plumer's rationale, see William Plumer's manuscript "Autobiography," June 27, 1817, Roll LC4, 352–53, William Plumer Papers, Library of Congress and the New Hampshire Historical Society (microfilm, New Hampshire Historical Society, Concord).

JOSEPH DYER, A *Compendious Narrative*

1. The whipped child is Orville Dyer.

2. Benjamin Putnam was a Freewill Baptist minister who had preached since the age of fourteen. He baptized Mary and Joseph Dyer and several of their neighbors in 1809.

3. Joseph alludes to 2 Timothy 3:6. Interestingly, the anti-Shaker author Daniel Rathbun makes the same reference, although he casts the Shaker leaders in the role of the deceivers of silly, sin-filled women. See Rathbun, *A Letter from Daniel Rathbun*, 101.

4. "Friends" refers to Mary's family, including her mother and several siblings who lived in Northumberland.

5. Crooker was the itinerant preacher who first brought news of Shakerism to the Dyers and their neighbors (see the introduction).

6. See note 5 to the text of *A Brief Statement*.

7. Joseph brought Betsey and Orville to the Shakers.

8. Mary accused the Shakers of secret, sexual improprieties (see note 17 to the text of *A Brief Statement*), and here Joseph responds, alleging that Mary attempted to convince Shakers to abandon gender segregation and celibacy in favor of paired, perhaps sexual, relationships. Joseph and Shaker leaders claimed that Mary referred to this as a "spiritual marriage"—a

relationship not sanctified by legal or civil ceremony—and that she argued that this practice would be acceptable for selected, leading Shakers. Although the details of Mary's alleged proposal are not clear, Joseph's accusation attempts to portray Mary as deviant, ignoring both mainstream conventions of legal marriage and the Shaker practice of celibacy and community-wide bonds. Mary Dyer was not the only proponent of change to Shaker practice. In the mid-nineteenth century several Shakers proposed a doctrine of "purified generation," arguing that pure love between a man and a women would replace the lust of original sin and thus permit sexual intercourse. Two such spiritually pure people could thus create pure offspring. At the Harvard, Massachusetts, Shaker community, Roxalana Grosvenor promoted this doctrine, often referred to as spiritual marriage, and was subsequently barred from the community. See the discussion in Suzanne R. Thurman, "O Sisters Ain't You Happy?": Gender, Family, and Community among the Harvard and Shirley Shakers, 1781–1918 (Syracuse: Syracuse University Press, 2002), 149–58.

9. These letters have not survived.
10. Mary Mills was an eldress of the Enfield North Family.
11. John Lyon was an elder of the Enfield North Family.
12. In the Old Testament, Potiphar's wife attempts to seduce Joseph, a son of Jacob and Rachel who had been sold into slavery in Egypt by his jealous brothers. When he refuses her, she falsely accuses him, and Potiphar, an Egyptian officer of the Pharoah, has him jailed (Genesis 39). In this reference, Joseph suggests both Mary's alleged wantoness and her proclivity to falsely accuse honorable Shakers with her own poor behavior.
13. Canterbury, New Hampshire, located just east of Concord, was the second of the two New Hampshire Shaker communities.
14. See note 17 to the text of A Brief Statement.
15. "It is well for a man not touch a woman. But because of the temptation to immorality, each man should have his own wife and each wife her own husband" (1 Corinthians 7:1–2). Paul continues with injunctions to remain faithful and to remain married.
16. Romans 1:26: "For this reason God gave them up to dishonorable passions. Their women exchanged natural relations for unnatural." Joseph accused Mary of making homosexual advances to Curtis.
17. Curtis's deposition is among the affidavits that follow A Compendious Narrative. She offered further elaborations of her statement in Mary's A Portraiture of Shakerism, the Shakers' Review of A Portraiture, and in Mary's Reply to a Review. Each subsequent deposition parsed ever more carefully her previous statements.

18. On this advertisement and the second one, mentioned below, see the introduction.

19. Edmund Lougee was an elder of the North Family.

20. Joseph and the elders are urging Mary to visit in the trustees' office, where business between Shakers and non-Shakers was conducted. By remaining in the North Family dwelling house, Mary is enacting what she sees as a wife's right to remain in her husband's (and by extension her) home, even if that home is within a Shaker village. Joseph, by insisting that Mary meet him at the trustees' office, is signaling that he no longer considers Mary a part of his Shaker family and that she is no longer welcome in the sacred space of Believers.

21. Coös County, in northern New Hampshire.

22. Moody Rich was Mary's brother-in-law, the husband of her sister Sally; his deposition is among those appended to Mary's *Brief Statement*.

23. On James Willis and his unsuccessful suit against Joseph Dyer, see the introduction.

24. Mary also purchased a half quire of paper on Joseph's account, perhaps to record her experiences and anti-Shaker sentiments.

25. Indenture was very common in the early nineteenth century. Families with slim economic resources, or those broken by the death of a parent, might indenture their children as a means of providing them with a more secure life. In the case of the Shakers, the sect would house, feed, clothe, educate, and train each indentured child in a gender-appropriate skill. At the age of majority, the child was free to join the community or leave. Historically, among the Shakers, the vast majority of indentured children left; the Dyer children were an exception. They were indentured to the Enfield Shakers by both Mary and Joseph Dyer on December 2, 1813, and then a second time by Joseph Dyer on March 27, 1816. Four of the five children remained Shakers until their deaths. On custody suits involving Shaker-held children see Barbara Taback Schneider, "Prayers for Our Protection and Prosperity at Court: Shakers, Children, and the Law," *Yale Journal of Law & the Humanities* 4 (1992): 33–78.

26. Betsey Dyer, in fact, became one of the first female trustees, or business leaders, at the Enfield Shaker community, a position she held until her death from tuberculosis in 1824.

27. Mary Dyer, "Friends of Humanity," *New Hampshire Patriot*, July 14, 1818.

28. Ann Lee was the founder of the Shakers, officially called the United Society of Believers in Christ's Second Appearing. Her brother William traveled with the original group of Shakers from England to the American colonies in 1774. Neither Ann nor William Lee passed through New Hampshire.

29. In this section, Joseph picks apart Mary's pamphlet *A Brief Statement*, with reference to specific pages—testimony that these two works were in dialogue with each other.
30. Joseph refers here to the preachers Benjamin Putnam and Lemuel Crooker.
31. Jewett was a member of the North Family at the Enfield Shaker community and one of the signers of the 1818 Remonstrance to Mary Dyer's legislative petition.
32. An 1814 appraisal of the Dyers' assets is recorded in Henry Blinn's history of the Enfield Shakers. The Dyers' property included 200 acres in Stewartstown valued at $800; additional land there worth $250; household furniture, cloth, and goods totaling $191.47; and notes and cash at $191.92. The total value was $1433.39. Blinn, *Historical Notes*, 106.
33. Arnold was the American Revolutionary War general who began fighting for the American Continental Army but in 1780 switched sides and joined the British army. While fighting for the colonists, he was made commander of the fort at West Point and attempted, unsuccessfully, to surrender the fort to the British.
34. Celsus was a second-century philosopher whose lost work *The True Word* opposed Christianity.
35. Jude 1:18–19 warns against false teachers.
36. The original of this letter does not survive.
37. This hymn, titled "The Faithful Few," is from the Shaker hymnal *Millennial Praises* (Part III, hymn 32) compiled by Seth Y. Wells and published in 1813. For a recent edition with introductory essays see Christian Goodwillie and Jane F. Crosthwaite, eds., *Millennial Praises: A Shaker Hymnal* (Amherst: University of Massachusetts Press, 2009).
38. *It is probable the reason why she pitched upon us is because we were members together in the Episcopal Church.* [Original note.]
39. See note 12.
40. Curtis is referring to Lemuel Crooker.
41. *See page 13, in a pamphlet entitled "the Sufferings of Mary Dyer."* [Original note.]
42. See note 17 to the text of *A Brief Statement*.
43. The grandmother is Zeruiah Harriman Marshall (1753–1842), a widow since 1800.
44. Caleb Dyer remained with the Enfield Shakers until his death, becoming the community's lead trustee and bringing great prosperity to the village. Among his many accomplishments was the building of the Great Stone Dwelling House, a six-story granite building that was the largest of all Shaker dwelling houses. It remains today on the site of the Enfield Shaker

village. Caleb died in 1863, shot by an aggrieved father attempting to re-
claim his children from the Shakers. On his life and death see *A Biography
of the Life and Tragical Death of Elder Caleb M. Dyer* (Manchester, N.H.:
American Steam Printing Works of Gage, Moore & Co., 1863), and Elizabeth A. De Wolfe, "Murder by Inches: Shakers, Family, and the Death of
Elder Caleb Dyer," in *Murder on Trial, 1620–2002*, ed. Robert Asher, Law-
rence B. Goodheart and Alan Rogers (Albany: State University of New
York Press, 2005), 185–206.

45. Betsey Dyer died from consumption (tuberculosis) in January 1824. Mary
Dyer learned of her daughter's death from a newspaper while lecturing and
selling books in Massachusetts. In her next anti-Shaker publication, she
highlighted the tragedy of a mother who lacked the resources to mourn
her dead child properly, and the pain of learning of Betsey's illness and
death after the fact stayed with her for decades. In the 1840s, she spear-
headed a massive petition asking the New Hampshire legislature (among
other demands) to force the Shakers to notify non-Shaker relatives when
a family member became ill in a Shaker community.

Of Mary and Joseph's remaining children, Joseph Jr. remained a Shaker
until his death in 1840 of an unknown cause. Orville became a much respected Shaker leader and served as elder of the Enfield Church Family for
twenty-eight years; he died in 1882. Jerrub, a physician, left the Shakers in
1852, married, and moved to Wisconsin. He later returned to New Hampshire where he raised a family (and, in 1867, buried his mother).

46. The *Remonstrance* was submitted to the New Hampshire legislature as a
rebuttal to Mary Dyer's claims. Caught off guard by Mary's *Brief Statement*,
the Shakers had little time to respond in print to her latest accusations.
The *Remonstrance* was published in the Concord, New Hampshire, newspapers and as a separate, slim, pamphlet, but it would be months before *A
Compendious Narrative* was ready for the public.

47. The poem is the text of the Shaker hymn "Gospel Liberty" (Part IV, hymn
28 of the collection *Millenial Praises* (see note 37 above). This poem cap-
tures the Shaker practice of using *yea* and *nay*, a tradition that continues
to present day.

INDEX

Elizabeth A. De Wolfe is a professor of history at the University of New England in Biddeford, Maine. She studied at Colgate University (B.A.), the University of New York at Albany (M.A.), and Boston University, from which she received her Ph.D. in American and New England studies. De Wolfe is the author of *Shaking the Faith: Women, Family, and Mary Marshall Dyer's Anti-Shaker Campaign, 1815–1867* (2002), which received the Communal Studies Association 2003 Outstanding Book Award. She is also the author of *The Murder of Mary Bean and Other Stories* (2007) which received several awards, including the 2008 Book Award from the New England Historical Association and the 2008 Peter C. Rollins Book Award from the Northeast Popular Culture/American Culture Association. With Thomas S. Edwards, De Wolfe coedited *Such News of the Land: U.S. Women Nature Writers* (2000). She lives in southern Maine with her husband, a rare book dealer.